Praise for *Releasing Leadership Brilliance*

"As a former small-plane pilot I was excited to see the book's flight metaphor and found it very accurate—for both flying and education! The emphasis on culture building and bringing out each person's brilliance responds perfectly to complaints regarding compliance and new initiatives. As Bailey and Reilly point out, by not focusing on what drags you down and focusing instead on what lifts you up and thrusts you forward, the brilliance of each individual in the educational community will shine."

Dr. Linda Gross, ***past co-author***
Consultant for Council of School Administrators
New York City, NY

"The book is an easy read full of excellent success stories. It offers a simple, easy-to-understand way to look at changes that can make a difference in student learning and student efficacy. I love the many references to a broad range of other books that help reinforce the points made."

Andy Tompkins, ***former Commissioner of Education***
Consultant for Regents Universities
Topeka, KS

"I'm glad someone took the time to study the Breakthrough Schools and clarify their secrets to success. I encourage leaders everywhere to use *Releasing Leadership Brilliance* to inspire new thinking and powerful actions. I highly recommend the organizer for addressing leadership as well as the case studies and exercises."

Stephanie Hirsh, ***Executive Director***
Learning Forward
Dallas, TX

"This book is about big change in our schools and how to make this change in all ZIP codes across the country. Its purpose is to help educational leaders soar, finding both personal and team brilliance. The stories shared are compelling and inspiring highlighting the powerful role of building principals who have transformed schools into places of learning where everyone thrives. The authors challenge educators, asking, 'Are your limiting beliefs creating barriers to reach your brilliance?' Anchored in solid research, but written from the viewpoint of caring, courageous, uplifting educators, this book is a must read."

Dayna Richardson, ***Executive Director***
Learning Forward
Hutchinson, KS

"A fanciful query into concise actions that can be used to create change in impactful ways. This book is a valuable guide to helping educators focus change that has the promise to spark improvement."

Billy Ray Jones, ***Supervising Principal***
South Jones High School
Ellisville, MS

"It's unbelievable that this compact book could hold so much information and examples in only four chapters. Great read! Great examples! This book is a call to action. I'm unable to read this book and not want to try something new."

Delsia Malone, ***Principal***
W. E. Striplin Elementary
Gadsden, AL

"*Releasing Leadership Brilliance* brings together work from several major educational researchers and cohesively forms practical strategies, techniques, and tools for educational leaders."

Glen Ishiwata, ***Retired Superintendent***
Moreland School District
San Jose, CA

"The language in the book speaks directly to educators. The book contains the right mix of fact, life, and guidance. The authors write with authenticity by virtue of having lived the experiences."

Neil MacNeill, ***Head Master***
Ellenbrook Independent Primary School
Ellenbrook, Western Australia

"Finally! This book successfully brings forth both theory and tools, with the passion that calls to educators who want to achieve better outcomes for ALL students. The stories of schools that have consistently improved…who have overcome the obstacles and stopped talking about barriers but rather removed them TOGETHER are powerful! This book offers so many suggestions for how to achieve great results in any school or district while highlighting the important point that all team members are leaders."

Lynn Lisy-Macan, ***Visiting Assistant Professor***
University at Albany-SUNY
Albany, NY

"This book is unique among books on leadership theory, change agency, and transformational change. Furthermore, it includes many tools to engage readers in the type of self-reflection that draws one into action."

Karen L. Tichy, ***Assistant Professor of Educational Leadership***
Saint Louis University
St. Louis, MO

"The quest to find our best selves, live our best lives, and shine with our own brilliance is the heart's desire of every human being. Two people compelled to help us find that pathway and acknowledge our brilliance have been divinely called. NASSP supports Great Leaders in every school who are committed to the success of each student. Through this commitment we provide resources to school leaders as they journey to develop themselves, their teachers, and their students. NASSP enthusiastically endorses this book and readily shared the stories of the leaders of our Breakthrough Schools to move Simon T. Bailey and Marceta F. Reilly's message of Brilliance forward. This book is a brilliant light."

Dr. Beverly Hutton, ***Deputy Executive Director/Chief Program Officer***
National Association of Secondary School Principals
Reston, VA

"What a fun, encouraging, doable, brilliant message for today's educators on their way to becoming champions for all! This book is an essential next step for those aspiring leaders who are stuck in the overwhelming rut of professional development. It is a brilliant way to expand our thinking into practical ways of having thoughtful conversations with staff, students, parents, and community. Building a leadership conversation around the metaphor of flight is another brilliant move, as is the use of success stories from all walks of life."

Joan Hearne, MEd, ACC Adjunct Professor, ***Former Principal/Coordinator of Staff Development***
Newman University and Wichita Public Schools
Wichita, KS

"Simon T. Bailey and Marceta F. Reilly have presented a gift of their combined wisdom, experience, and brilliance. Not only do they offer illuminating research and stories, but they have enriched and expanded the information with interviews of those who employ best practices. You will find ready-to-use tools and activities for professional learning and collaboration. If you are a busy leader looking for a new lift in your leadership, keep this book close in your day-to-day work for informative and practical resources, knowledge, and inspiration. Use it as the basis for fresh dialogue as you elevate your leadership and break sound barriers toward a brilliant education for all those you serve."

Diana Williams, ***Leadership Coach, Author and Chief of Evaluation Services***
Coaching for Results, Inc.
Columbus, OH

"Rarely are school leaders presented with a comprehensive leadership book that addresses all the players in the educational arena—the leader, community members, instructional staff, and students. The expertise shared by the authors—a business executive and a former superintendent/leadership coach—provide exercises, tools, and resources designed to break the sound barrier of limiting beliefs for each of these populations. The stories included from courageous school leaders offer hope to practitioners intent on using the expertise inside their system to bring lasting instructional change for all the students they serve. Bravo!"

Edna Harris, ***Co-author***
Results Coaching: The New Essential for School Leaders
Round Rock, TX

Releasing Leadership Brilliance

Releasing Leadership Brilliance

Breaking Sound Barriers in Education

Simon T. Bailey
Marceta F. Reilly

Foreword by Russell J. Quaglia

A Joint Publication

FOR INFORMATION:

Corwin
A SAGE Company
2455 Teller Road
Thousand Oaks, California 91320
(800) 233-9936
www.corwin.com

SAGE Publications Ltd.
1 Oliver's Yard
55 City Road
London EC1Y 1SP
United Kingdom

SAGE Publications India Pvt. Ltd.
B 1/I 1 Mohan Cooperative Industrial Area
Mathura Road, New Delhi 110 044
India

SAGE Publications Asia-Pacific Pte. Ltd.
3 Church Street
#10-04 Samsung Hub
Singapore 049483

Executive Editor: Arnis Burvikovs
Senior Associate Editor: Desirée A. Bartlett
Editorial Assistant: Kaitlyn Irwin
Production Editor: Amy Schroller
Copy Editor: Diana Breti
Typesetter: Hurix Systems Pvt. Ltd.
Proofreader: Jeff Bryant
Indexer: Rick Hurd
Cover Designer: Paul Vorreiter
Marketing Manager: Anna Mesick

Printed in the United States of America

ISBN 978-1-5063-4696-0

This book is printed on acid-free paper.

17 18 19 20 21 10 9 8 7 6 5 4 3 2 1

Contents

Use the Aurasma app to access video clips on the front and back cover of the book. You can access additional video clips from the authors at www.releasingleadershipbrilliance.com.

Foreword

Simon and Marceta remind us that there is more than one way to understand and appreciate the dynamic forces at work in education. They introduce educational leaders to the metaphor of aviation to connect the dynamics of flying to the dynamics of leading. Concepts such as *weight*, *lift*, *thrust*, and *drag* provide readers with a new mindset for leadership. Little did I realize that I would truly learn how to "fly," not in flight school but by reading their book about leadership in education! This book is about what it takes for schools—and everyone who works in them—to take off ... or, in aspirational terms, be able to dream and set goals for the future while being inspired in the present to reach your everyday brilliance!

Releasing Leadership Brilliance does more than provide a framework for transforming schools; it provides concrete examples and resources that are essential to effectively allow all individuals to fly and be brilliant. The real-life case studies are examples of success that allow readers to understand the type of fuel it takes for an entire educational community to take flight with passion and a commitment to sustainable transformation. The exercises included in each chapter assist readers in reflecting on the current state of their own leadership and their schools and help them assess the most effective way forward.

Data from the Quaglia School Voice Surveys indicates that in order to move forward *together*, leaders must be willing to listen to and learn from members of the school community. When stakeholders have a voice in the school improvement process, they increase their sense of self-worth, are meaningfully engaged, and above all, have a genuine sense of purpose. The *School Voice Report 2016* shows that students who agree that they have a voice in school are seven times more likely to report they are academically motivated than students who do not agree with those Student Voice statements. Similarly, the national teacher data demonstrate that when teachers have a voice, they are more motivated and more positive about their influential role as teachers. The report shows that when teachers believe that building administration is open to new ideas and/or willing to learn from staff, they are two to four times more likely to value setting goals, to work hard to reach their goals, and to have positive feelings about their ability to make a difference as a teacher. Clearly, if leadership brilliance is to be realized, the voices of all in education need to be heard and valued.

Not only does incorporating voice in school transformation positively impact those providing input, but it simultaneously ensures that decisions are based on information gathered from the very individuals with firsthand experience in schools. What better feedback is there to help reduce drag? As you consider professional development at your school, remember that just as your student body changes each year, so should your teacher training. Brilliant leaders make it a point to listen and learn from teachers and students—determine what the existing needs are and establish professional development that addresses those needs. Meaningful, relevant professional development that responds to the voice of stakeholders is critical for sustainable transformation.

Simon and Marceta have high expectations of you as a reader. (And they should, just as there should be high expectations for teachers and students!) As you read this book, you should be prepared to self-reflect, examine your own beliefs and goals for the school, and commit to collaborating with others to determine effective ways to improve student achievement. Always remember that leadership is a collaborative journey, one where individuals should feel valued for their unique talents, ideas, and insights. I have found the most effective approach for this is the School Voice Model: Listen, Learn, and Lead, as explained in *Principal Voice* (Quaglia, 2016). Having voice as a leader is about taking action: *listening* to the voices of those around you, *learning* from the thoughts and ideas of others, and *leading* toward a shared goal—all the while respecting and supporting others through the journey. Using your voice, in a collaborative leadership role, will allow you to foster the ability of everyone in your school to reach their fullest potential. This action-oriented approach resonates in the *Releasing Leadership Brilliance* journey, where collaboration and teamwork underscore the ability to release the individual and collective brilliance throughout your school!

This book challenges you to evaluate yourself first, reflect on your own beliefs, and assess how you conduct yourself as a leader. Armed with this knowledge, you can unlock your own potential. With a commitment to improving your own leadership skills, you can then invite others to begin their journeys. With a shared belief in the goals of the school, these journeys can merge to inspire and engage students, colleagues, and community members alike. When your school environment is filled with individuals who are committed to reducing drag and engaging students, then students have the opportunity to soar. Isn't that why we all became educators in the first place—to help every individual reach his or her fullest potential?

I know the next time I am sitting on a runway preparing for take-off to another school district, I will have a completely different mindset when the pilot says, "We are number one for takeoff!" My seatbelt will be fastened, and I will be better prepared to create *lift* in schools, thanks to Simon and Marceta.

—Russell J. Quaglia

Acknowledgments

We would like say thank you to Jayne Warrilow for being the brilliant connector who brought us together. We are forever grateful for you imparting your sage wisdom into our lives.

Thank you to Melissa Spencer for coordinating hectic schedules between two busy people. We celebrate your administrative brilliance. Denise Milligan, thank you for sharing your business strategies with us and being our cheerleader in this process. Gennia Holder, thank you for using your technology brilliance to ensure that we made use of all the social media tools to get this book out into the world.

Our editor, Arnis Burvikovs, you are brilliant, and thank you for recognizing the potential of our book. Thank you for prodding, encouraging, coaching, and guiding our work.

Thank you to Desirée Bartlett, Anne Mesick, Rose Storey, Andrew Olson, Kaitlyn Irwin, Amy Schroller, and the rest of the Corwin team for championing our work and patiently helping us bring our ideas to life. You are consummate professionals and one of the finest publishers we've ever worked with in the world.

Dr. Beverly Hutton, you are one of the finest human beings we know. Thank you for believing in our book and introducing us to the NASSP. We cherish our relationship and look forward to our collaboration in the days ahead.

Joan Auchter, the first time we met you at the NASSP offices there was an instant connection. You resonated with our vision for transforming the mindsets of educators and graciously shared your seasoned insights. Thank you.

Josephine Franklin, you are one of the kindest people we've ever met. We are forever thankful to you for accepting our conference calls, face-to-face meetings, e-mails, and questions regarding the Breaking Ranks® framework. Our book wouldn't be what it is today without your input. Bravo!

Sue Pepe and Carol Fetzer, you strongly encouraged us to include stories of NAESP in our book. Well, we did it and the book is so much richer because of your suggestion.

Dr. Barbara Jenkins, thank you for listening, motivating, and leading by example. Pam Gould and Kat Gordon, you are some of the finest school board members in public education. Orange County Public School students and parents are better because of your brilliant imprint.

Thank you to all of the inspiring principals and school leaders who were interviewed for this book. You rock!

Paul Vorreiter, WOW…is all that we can say for designing a book cover that we love. Susan Wranick, thank you for helping shape our keynote presentation.

Thank you to the brilliant Corwin authors who, without hesitation, answered our survey questions, accepted our conference calls, and answered our follow-up questions. We are forever grateful for your kindness and the difference you are making in the world.

Publisher's Acknowledgments

Corwin would like to recognize the following individuals for taking the time to provide their editorial insight and guidance:

Glen Ishiwata, Retired Superintendent
Moreland School District
San Jose, CA

Billy Ray Jones, Principal and Student Voice Consultant
South Jones High School
Ellisville, MS

Lynn Lisy-Macan, Visiting Assistant Professor
University at Albany-SUNY
Albany, NY

Neil MacNeill, Head Master
Ellenbrook Independent Primary School
Ellenbrook, Western Australia

Delsia Malone, Principal
W. E. Striplin Elementary School
Gadsden, AL

Karen Ray, Director of Professional Learning and Advanced Academics
Eagle Mountain-Saginaw ISD
Fort Worth, TX

Karen L. Tichy, Assistant Professor of Educational Leadership
Saint Louis University
St. Louis, MO

About the Authors

Simon T. Bailey is attempting to put a dent in the universe. He is a guy from inner-city Buffalo, New York, who currently resides in Orlando, Florida. He leads an educational company whose purpose is to teach one billion people how to be brilliant in life and business. He is the former sales director of Disney Institute and one of America's top 10 most-booked corporate and association speakers. He is the proud father of two awesome teenagers. He loves movies and cheers on the Buffalo Bills, who will win a Super Bowl in his lifetime!

Marceta F. Reilly is a thought leader and passionate advocate for creating schools and districts in which everybody—students, staff, parents, community—thrives. She spent 34 years of her career in public education experimenting with ways to teach and lead that make schools the trusted center (the heart!) of a community. Now she spends her time as an author, speaker, and leadership coach for educators across the United States. Marceta and her husband have two daughters and six brilliant grandchildren. She loves traveling, wine tasting, and keeping up with the grandkids as their lives unfold.

To my brilliant gems—Daniel and Madison, you are the wind beneath my wings. I love you and believe in you.

And

To Ms. Rosa Stephens, Mrs. Rita Lankes, Dorothy Buchanan, and Alpha Kappa Alpha Sorority, Inc., and all the educators who polished me when I was a diamond in the rough.

—Simon

To all educators and children—you are our future! Dream big! Be bold! Have confidence and courage to create a "justice-seeking, earth-honoring, self-respecting" world for all of us.

And

To my grandchildren in particular—you are the reason I do what I do! You give me hope and dreams of a world where everybody thrives. I love you all!

—Marceta

Introduction

Applying the Physics of Flight to the Educational System

Our Rationale: The Big "Why?"

Zappos Founder and CEO Tony Hsieh unveiled his plan for reinventing his organization about a year ago. He told his staff that, effective immediately, there would be no more people managers and that the new approach would "require fewer roles that primarily . . . drive alignment across legacy silos" (McGregor, 2015). He went on to say that going forward there would be a new world order—self-management.

Zappos, an Amazon-owned company, has always been a risk-taking culture. What started as a fledging hope, a dream, and a wish to sell shoes via the Internet—and the first website to offer free shipping—has made them successful. At the helm is Tony Hsieh, a leader clearly uncomfortable with the status quo and willing to mix it up for the sake of doing something fresh and different.

However, often when organizations attempt to do something radical, they are met with dogmatic resistance to change and the possibility of utter failure. There are no promises that it will work out. And indeed, Hsieh's organization has been turned upside down. But Hsieh says, "The one thing I'm absolutely sure of is that the future is about self-management" (Reingold, 2016).

We believe that you, like Hsieh, have the ability to raise the bar on the results for your system. As a leader, what are you willing to do that has never been done before? Will you have the courage to take bold steps, even when you don't know the exact outcome? Will you do it?

As we read Hsieh's radical approach to disrupting his organization, we couldn't help but think about the seminal work of Thomas Friedman, *The World Is Flat,* in which he forecasts a disappearing middle-management layer coming to organizations as a result of automation and other global flatteners.

These same kinds of change winds are blowing through the education sector. It sometimes seems that everyone *outside the system* is telling education how to change. They say it needs to be leaner, more collaborative, more focused on the needs of individual children. That may be true, but we believe that *educators* are the best ones to be leading this kind of transformational change in our schools.

But there is no reason for educational leaders to feel nervous about this kind of future. In this new way of thinking, every committed leader has the opportunity to be a spark who, like Hsieh and Friedman, intentionally sets about breaking the sound barriers of limiting beliefs and helps lead us into an era of educational brilliance.

Purpose of Our Book

The purpose of our book is to help you soar as an educational leader who

- Understands the "weight" and power of your calling;
- Works with others to create "lift" in the system;
- Provides "thrust" for teams to move forward;
- And most important, "reduces drag" so that *students* can soar.

Our book offers educators a framework that includes easy exercises, simple tools, and relevant resources to enhance their work of transforming their schools.

- Educators will evaluate how they are showing up as leaders and learn to inspire the type of environment they want to create.
- They will learn to look for self-limiting beliefs and build consensus around meaningful goals that tap into the strengths of individuals within the community.
- They will learn ways to improve teachers' ability to work together in teams in order to produce greater achievement among students.

- They will learn to increase teacher commitment by focusing on breaking down barriers to learning and inspiring students to blossom as they engage in learning.

But even more than that, our purpose in writing this book is to engage and equip educational leaders to break their "sound barriers" of limiting beliefs and bureaucracy. We want to improve schools and school districts across America and the world. Our vision is to instill the mindset to change yourself first and then change the system that you are in. We want this book to provide the spark that shifts educators' thinking and propels them into action that will take them through implementation to delivery of the promise of education as a pathway for students out of poverty and into reaching their full potential.

Background for the Flight Metaphor

Sir Ken Robinson, author, educator, and creativity expert, tells us that the dropout rate in some of our schools, particularly those in high-poverty communities, is 60% or more. Some economists estimate that, if we cut that number in half, the net gain to the U.S. economy over the next 10 years would be nearly $1 trillion! (Robinson, 2013).

But that is just the tip of the iceberg. It does not take into consideration all the students who are disengaged, don't enjoy school, and don't benefit from it. Yet in the United States, we spend more money than most countries on education, often have smaller class sizes, and spend hundreds of thousands of dollars on new initiatives each year to improve. So why aren't we getting better results?

We believe it is because of "sound barriers" in our thinking about education. As you may already know, a sound barrier refers to the point at which an aircraft moves from transonic to supersonic speed. In the 1940s, an aircraft would experience compression that struck the plane, thereby preventing it from further acceleration. Scientists believed that the drag on the aircraft caused by the approaching speed made it impossible for it to reach or exceed the speed of sound without being destroyed. But in the 1950s, through advancing technology, aircraft were able to effortlessly break the sound barrier.

Today's global economy has been sputtering along as it attempts to regain a normal speed. Many people have been sidelined because of the "sound barriers" of no jobs, depleted retirement accounts, empty houses lost in foreclosure, subpar living, and even homelessness. As a result, many people have bought into fear and lost hope. That "sound barrier" is equivalent to being left behind in life, and it blocks them from breaking through to their next dimension of possibility or, even for some, their desire for the American dream.

Each school year, parents entrust their children to a school system that is supposed to prepare them for a better future. But in many of our communities, this dream for our schools has died because of an artificial mental barrier of hopelessness. This blocks students and teachers from breaking through the sound barriers of limiting beliefs to the next dimension of possibility. Educators simply stop searching for budding great artists, painters, musicians, lawyers, doctors, preachers, engineers, scientists, writers, and politicians from among the children. Instead, they settle for obedience and compliance. The challenges and social fabric seem just too hard to change.

But now as you look around the world, we are experiencing a new generation of thinking that is breaking the sound barrier in the blink of an eye. We are seeing and sensing what psychologists call a new "set point" or mindset. In his book *The Greatest Secret*, Ron McIntosh tells a classic story. In 1953, no runner had ever run a mile in less than four minutes. In fact, many thought it was impossible. However, Roger Bannister believed it could be done, and in 1954, he became the first man to break the four-minute mile barrier.

"Once Bannister did it, someone else broke his record within one month. Before the end of the year, six others broke the four-minute mile. Within another year, 60 people had broken the barrier," says Ron. He goes on to say, "When people thought it was impossible, it *was* impossible. When a man believed in his heart and changed his thinking, what was considered to be impossible became possible" (McIntosh, 2007).

Here in America, we are at a critical juncture where educational leaders are being invited to break the sound barrier of providing an average educational experience to creating a consistently brilliant educational experience. We are asking educators to create a new sound and *become* the breakthrough in their schools, communities, and nation. When leaders break sound barriers, they create the conditions for new ideas and practices to take root and flourish.

The Journey to Break Sound Barriers

The content of our book is organized around the metaphor of the four forces of flight—weight, lift, thrust, and drag. When leaders understand these forces, they can overcome the "sound barriers" of educational inertia.

- ***Weight*** is the force of gravity toward the center of the earth. We use this to talk about unleashing *Personal Brilliance* through self-discovery: Who am I as a leader? What do I believe?
- ***Lift*** is the force that acts at a right angle to the direction of motion. We use this to talk about expanding *Collaborative Brilliance* to engage and energize our stakeholders: How can we become more than 1 + 1 = 2?
- ***Thrust*** is the force that propels a flying machine in the direction of motion. Engines produce the thrust. We use this to talk about leaders becoming the engine for *Team Brilliance* by encouraging smart risks and designing potent changes: What works?
- ***Drag*** is the force of resistance that acts opposite to the relative motion of any moving object. It slows down and impedes acceleration. We use this to talk about how to reframe and clear blocks to *Student Brilliance:* How do we unleash grit, resilience, and hope in students? What is limiting us? So what? Now what?

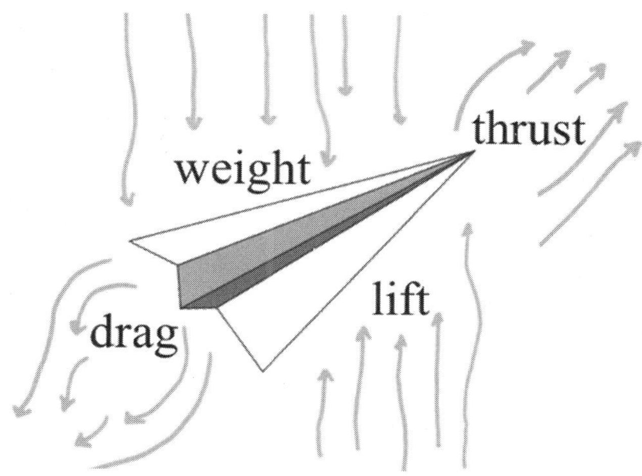

In the book, we not only make the case for change, we provide tools and exercises in each chapter that educators can use to move the chapter ideas into implementation in relevant, concrete ways.

To accomplish this design, we use a storytelling format. Each section tells one or more powerful stories/case studies, explains concepts in an easy-to-understand way, offers implementation tools and exercises, and calls you, the reader, to specific action in order to make progress.

Each section of the book contributes to a system or learning curriculum for the reader. If you follow the system and do the work, you will begin to move your school in the direction of the promise of education: tapping into student curiosity, engaging students in schoolwork they love, and reaping benefits in high student achievement.

The Research Base for Our Book

The core of our research about what works is drawn from a large database of schools recognized in the Breakthrough Schools Project sponsored by the National Association of Secondary School Principals (NASSP) and MetLife. In 2007, NASSP and MetLife formed a partnership to identify outstanding examples of how determined and focused middle and high school principals create and sustain school improvement. Each year since then, NASSP has identified and named 10 schools as "Breakthrough Schools." The research this project has spawned is known as *Breaking Ranks*®.

The keystones of the *Breaking Ranks*® research fall into three core areas:

- Collaborative leadership, including professional learning communities and strategic use of data;
- Personalization of the school environment so that every student feels connected to his or her learning; and
- Curriculum, instruction, and assessment that are aligned with state and local standards.

We found many examples of how to implement deep change in schools by reading about and interviewing principals from the Breakthrough Schools recognized by NASSP and National Distinguished Principals recognized by the National Association of Elementary School Principals. In addition, we have included stories from Simon's experiences working with school districts he has visited in his speaking tours and keynote addresses around the world. And Marceta brings stories of successful experiences from her own career and of clients with whom she works.

What the Authors Bring to This Book

Simon T. Bailey is renowned worldwide as an inspirational keynote speaker and thought leader in the area of leadership. He has broad and deep experience working at the executive level in several Fortune 500 companies. He is collaborating with Dr. Marceta Reilly, who has a 40-year career in education, moving from teacher through superintendent and leadership coach. She, too, is a rising thought leader in the reform movement. Together they combine their unique perspectives in business and education to equip leaders to make substantive and deep internal changes to our educational systems everywhere so that *all* students truly are able to reach their full potential as human beings.

Releasing Leadership Brilliance builds on Simon T. Bailey's earlier work, *Release Your Brilliance* (2008). Its premise is that every person is a diamond in the rough, holding something very precious inside that has the potential to reflect and bestow value. In the original book, readers learned how to tap into their core talents and shine for the world to see.

Marceta Reilly's earlier work with co-author Linda Gross Cheliotes, *Coaching Conversations: Transforming Your School One Conversation at a Time* (2010), also informs this work. Its premise is that by using coaching conversations, a school leader can change the climate, culture, and commitment within the school. The book focuses on teaching practical communication skills to help educators build strong, trusting relationships with staff and community.

In *Releasing Leadership Brilliance,* they are advocating that readers develop the mindset to disrupt the status quo and transform their environments to positively impact their schools. Educators will find tangible insights, case studies, and real-life examples of how schools like theirs have moved from mediocrity to brilliance by rolling up their sleeves and applying new transformational principles to old problems.

We expect our readers will be educators who

- Are seeking significant ways to create changes in their schools that result in improved student achievement;
- Want to communicate effectively and have an impact on their colleagues;

- Dream of influencing the policies and processes within their districts that will really make a difference for students and families; and
- Want to feel valued by the system for the experience and wisdom they bring to new initiatives.

Our Invitation to Come Fly With Us

We invite readers who are school leaders at all levels—principals and administrators, teachers, school boards, parents, and community leaders—to come "fly" with us. We are especially targeting school principals who are struggling to make their schools places of learning and aspiration for the students and communities they serve.

More than just a book, we want to present an educational template for leaders to use worldwide. Our vision is to instill the mindset in leaders to change oneself first and then change the system.

We can do this if we work together throughout the education world that will transform our schools into places of learning where *everybody* thrives—students, teachers, parents, and communities—by tapping into individual and collective brilliance.

Before you turn another page, visit the community website at **www.releasingleadershipbrilliance.com** to sign up for the downloadable starter kit that will get you started on transforming your school into a place of collective brilliance. The starter kit will include an FAQ section, book study questions, and more. On the website, in addition to the starter kit, you will find:

- More information about the authors;
- The RLB blog where you can comment and communicate with fellow readers;
- Additional resources;
- **Chapter-by-chapter videos giving additional insights on the themes of the book;**
- Steps on how to subscribe to the RLB community for monthly webinars, additional videos, podcasts, and other resources;
- Links for scheduling speaking engagements and workshops with the authors; and
- Candid snapshots of the authors—including Simon's first visit to Marceta's farm.

Return to the website regularly for new blog posts, comments from the RLB community, and updated resources. Get ready to be brilliant!

Personal Brilliance—Knowing Yourself Gives You "Weight" for Flight

Who Am I? The Problem That Creates Urgency

Simon tells the story about why he is so driven to impact education:

One of my joys when I am home is to drive my children to school. I look forward to it because my parents were not able to do it for me because they were working to put food on the table.

My son, Daniel, is a brilliant 16-year-old tenth-grader. Thank goodness he's not pushing to drive just yet. When I am not traveling, sometimes I have the privilege of driving him to school, and one morning on the way to school at 6:45 AM I tried to strike up a conversation.

Me: "How's it going?"

Daniel: "Dad, it's just another day."

That's it. No excitement, zero pep, and joyless energy.

Now I know that my son is quiet and unassuming, but there must be something to look forward to. I know that he works really hard in school and by no means was I comparing his response to my high school experience. It just seemed to me that he was coasting through another day.

In an instant I felt the hair on the back of my neck stand up and my heart skip a beat. I was a product of a Catholic and public school education in the third poorest city in America—Buffalo, NY. I started working at 12 years of age for my godfather who owned 40 rental properties throughout the city.

But here was my son who was living in the best ZIP code in Orlando, Florida, receiving a private school education paid for by his parents with no discounts or assistance, and the best he could muster up was, "It's just another day."

As we were driving along, I looked in his eyes and could see the life being sucked out of him because there was no expectation or anticipation to learn or discover anything that would shift his thinking. He was doing what he was told to do because everyone gets an education. But I was wondering what he was learning. As a father, and taxpayer, it scared the living daylights out of me.

After dropping him off, I came back home because I wanted to take Madison, our brilliant 13-year-old eighth-grade daughter, to the local public school for an Honors Math tutoring session to keep her sharp and STEM ready!

On the way to school I started the same kind of conversation with her.

Me: "What is your favorite part of school?"

Madison: "Seeing my friends."

I tried my best to keep a poker face and not drive off the road. Then I pressed in a little more, to make sure that I heard her correctly.

Me: "What else do you like about school?"

Madison: "I love 7th period."

Me: "Why?"

Madison: "Because it's science class and the teacher always makes it fun. We get to discover new things."

WOW…now that was a very interesting response.

Then I decided to flip the question and asked, "What don't you like about school?"

Without hesitation, my 13-year-old focus group of one said, "School is boring and not fun at all."

Now, here is where I start channeling my inner Liam Neeson, who played the driven father in the movie Taken. *I am doing my best to connect with my daughter, only to realize that her curiosity for learning is dying a slow death. When she was 8 years of age, she tested as gifted, but now at 13 years of age, and despite being put in eighth-grade honors math and science, she's bored and not having fun at school.*

Was this a phase she was going through? Did I drop the ball as a parent?

What was even more of a shocker to me is that both Daniel and Madison made the honor roll, thanks to their mother, who has a take-no-prisoners attitude when it comes to grades. Yet school was nothing special to them. They could take it or leave it.

This lack of joy for learning really concerned him. Simon realized his kids were graduating into a world where school, both public and private, trained them to take standardized tests but not to think critically so they could compete in the global marketplace. Instead, they were being shaped by a system that prided itself on conformity, standardization, and big data.

I'm not blaming the school, nor am I pointing fingers at the system. As Sir Ken Robinson has noted in a recent TED talk, "If you're a teacher, for your students *you are the system.* If you're a school principal, for your community *you are the system.* If you're a policymaker, for the schools you control *you are the system*" (Robinson, 2013).

Most parents and citizens try to do their part to educate and prepare their kids at home. They want them to be successful in the bigger world. But when we bring our best to the system, no matter what shape that is, we want them to become better, not duller. We don't want them to develop the perception that education is boring. That attitude can become a sound barrier that limits success.

So the question we have to ask is, *Does the system support educators who are passionate about what they do? Do educators feel they are doing significant work? Do they feel and sense the* weight *of the calling in their lives?*

The Relationship Between Weight and Personal Brilliance

Weight is the force of gravity toward the center of the earth. It is what gives an object mass and substance. It helps define the object for us. According to the Smithsonian National Air and Space Museum, there are four principles of flight: weight, lift, thrust, and drag. While lift, thrust, and drag are all "mechanical forces" generated by the interaction between an object and a liquid or gas, weight is a "field force." A field force does not have to be in physical contact with an object to have an effect on it.

For humans, this kind of field force has everything to do with our attitude and thinking. Our weight (how we think and feel about ourselves) can either build us up or tear us down.

Carter G. Woodson (2008), who wrote *The Mis-Education of the Negro,* states:

> If you can control a man's thinking you do not have to worry about his action. When you determine what a man shall think you do not have to concern yourself about what he will do. If you make a man feel that he is inferior, you do not have to compel him to accept an inferior status, for he will seek it himself. If you make a man think that he is justly an outcast, you do not have to order him to the back door. He will go without being told.

Often in education there is a pull from the system to remain average and to stick with the status quo. Powerful field forces lower the bar of what teachers expect from themselves and their students. These forces emerge from system politics, distrust of authorities, standardization of testing, frustration about the pace of change, fear of independent thinking, risk aversion, and playing it safe. No one wants to be an outlier, and those who speak up often have their wings clipped and then they surrender to the invisible power of these forces.

Educators can have all that is needed to soar to heights unknown, but if the weight created by the system overpowers them, then it causes a downward spiral, which leads to disengagement, discouragement, and disintegration of their brilliance.

In leadership, we see *weight* as the substance, grounding, and presence a person brings to the table. It can generate either positive or negative energy, depending upon the attitude, beliefs, and behaviors of individuals.

When it is positive energy, we call it *Personal Brilliance*. It starts by knowing your authentic self as a person and then as an educator, discovering what core values and beliefs frame who you are, and establishing your cornerstones for living. This *weight* grounds you and helps you show up confident, competent, and courageous in your work. It inspires others to bring their best selves to every situation.

We believe that who you are is more important than what you do. Your belief system shapes your future and impacts everyone around you. Your journey to personal brilliance begins with looking at the core of your soul. What drives you? What motivates you? What is it about education that captures your heart?

Personal Brilliance comes from finding your inner spark. When you are investing your abilities in something meaningful and congruent with your internal wiring, it creates a spark. That spark is a quality that causes your energy and joy to activate everyone around you.

Personal brilliance also comes from harnessing your presence. You do this by looking at yourself and considering how you intend to *be* before you *say* or *do* the work of leading others. This doesn't mean that you slack off in preparing substantive content. But researchers generally agree that 60% or more of what you communicate is delivered by your presence. So investing significant time in working on your self-awareness and being-ness is essential to developing your own positive *weight* and personal brilliance.

In the end, personal brilliance starts with understanding and changing yourself before you try to change anyone else.

As an educational leader, do you have that spark? Do you have a burning desire to shape the future by unlocking the potential inside young minds? Or have your wings been clipped by the headwinds of the system?

Unfortunately, some educators never soar because it's safer to stay in conformity. Conformity keeps educators from stepping into their full potential. They may think they are safe and comfortable, but failing to soar often causes them to feel drained and, in some cases, cynical.

We believe that when educators understand that these kinds of barriers are made to be broken, they will harness the positive forces of weight through their personal presence. That is when educators create a "BOOM."

Let us explain "BOOM." Tobias Rossmann (2002), a research engineer with Advanced Projects Research and a visiting researcher at the California Institute of Technology, explained that as the speed of an object increases to sonic velocity, the sound waves begin to pile up in front of the object. If the object has sufficient acceleration, it can burst through this barrier of sound waves and is heard on the ground as an explosion, or sonic boom. In October of 1947, U.S. Air Force Captain Charles E. "Chuck" Yeager became the first human to fly faster than the speed of sound (della Cava, 2012).

As Chuck Yeager sparked the "boom" that changed the history of flight, your leadership brilliance can become a "boom" to change your school system. It is about creating a "boom" that establishes a school culture of high trust and enthusiastic collaboration. It's about becoming a "boom" in classrooms by challenging students to reach for excellence. It's about developing a "boom" in your community that supports and energizes families to help ALL children thrive.

How do you do it? Accelerate past the inhibiting forces of inertia and instead use the positive forces of self-knowledge and core beliefs to become the agent of change in the classroom and beyond.

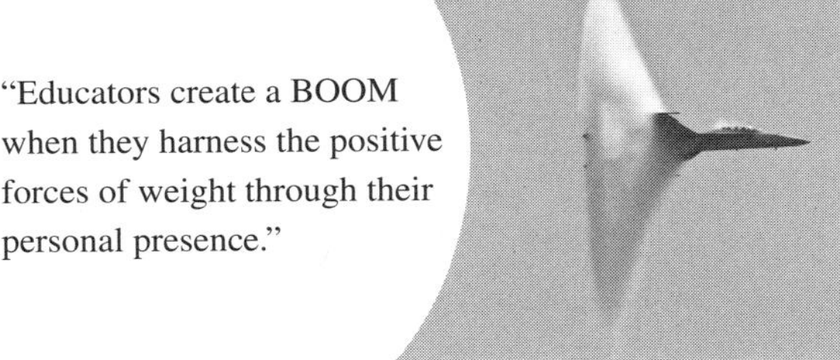

Break Your Sound Barrier: Real Examples From Real Educators

This is a story about Carol Conklin-Spillane who *grew into* her self-knowledge as she began her first leadership assignment as a principal at Sleepy Hollow High School in Sleepy Hollow, NY.

Her school was recognized as a Breakthrough School in 2014. But 22 years ago, things were quite different. Prior to her assignment, no principal had survived at the school for more than four years. Attendance policies were stacked against students in favor of hard rules and regulations that often made getting needed credits for graduation very difficult. Many school practices favored teacher interests rather than student needs. With the parade of principals before her, union contract rules filled the vacuum for leadership.

Carol was undaunted by what she found at the school. She intuitively understood that leadership starts with one's own mindset. And with her strong teaching background, she believed in sharing leadership, personalizing learning for students, and the power of good professional learning.

So she started the school turnaround by using the tools that she had available through union contracts to take the first steps into changing the culture. At the first faculty meeting, she asked lots of questions and listened deeply. She looked at where people sat, who spoke, who the power brokers were. Then she negotiated a deal with union leaders to change faculty meeting times from the contractual one hour per month *each* for faculty meetings and for department meetings to one and a half hours per month for faculty meetings only. In lieu of departmental meetings, she promised to be available five days per week after school for anybody who had questions or concerns they wanted to discuss with her.

Then she did a survey of staff to see what their learning needs were and began to use the faculty meeting time for professional learning. She changed the seating arrangements in the meeting room to show how learning could be collaborative and cooperative. She clustered the naysayers into one group so that information from reports that came from the different faculty groups was proportional and other perspectives could be heard.

Carol modeled new teaching ideas in the faculty meetings. She listened to teacher insights and what motivated them. She recruited teachers to try out new ideas and added enticements for them to work with her. For instance, she conducted voluntary book studies and collaborated with the members to discuss the ideas, experiment with them, share their experiences broadly with their colleagues, and become experts in the topics.

In this way, Carol started small and spread it big. It was a grassroots effort developing teachers using a show me/follow me model. As a result, she grew expertise and leadership from within the faculty and created a climate of interest and change for the school. She also modeled how she wanted teachers to build relationships with students (Conklin-Spillane, 2016).

Now Carol is retiring after 22 years as principal at the school. She has been recruited to become superintendent at a small neighboring school district. To that new role she will apply the lessons she has learned from her experience at Sleepy Hollow. It is embodied in her favorite quote by Haim Ginott (1972):

> I am the decisive element in the classroom. It is my personal approach that creates the climate. It is my daily mood that makes the weather.

This next story is about Tracy Smith, who found his personal brilliance mid-career through self-discovery. Tracy Smith was principal at West Bourbon Elementary in a rural school district in Kansas and became a coaching client of Marceta through a project with his regional service center.

Tracy had been very successful in many different roles in his school district—teacher, coach, principal. After 30-plus years, he was beloved by students, respected by teachers, and trusted by the community. Now he was eyeing retirement. But with two more years left on his contract to reach early retirement for pension benefits, he came to Marceta feeling burned out and empty. He had lost the fire in his belly. He figured this was just the way life was. He'd had a good life, put his mark on the school district, and would coast to the end. The best was all behind him.

But Tracy learned "that ain't necessarily so," as the Gershwin lyrics go. A regional grant offered leadership coaching for interested principals and superintendents. Curious about what the process was like, Tracy decided to sign up. Being a cooperative person, he humored Marceta by agreeing to do some self-discovery exercises.

Almost immediately his energy and attitude changed. Before, he had a vague sense of his core values, but after completing a values exercise, he was crystal clear about what really motivated (and triggered!) him. When he crafted his life purpose statement, he immediately felt renewed energy and direction for his work ahead.

However, he was transformed when he named his Four Cornerstones of great leadership—the four characteristics he believes make a truly great leader. He no longer wanted to coast. He was on fire about leaving a legacy of ethics, caring, and compassion that would last well beyond his tenure in the district.

Tracy was no longer willing to hide behind the veil of "good enough." He wanted to dream big and inspire his staff to their own greatness with students.

Instead of coasting through the last two years of his leadership, Tracy moved his staff to see more for themselves and their students than before. Working together, the school won the National Blue Ribbon Award for Excellence at the end of the year. The student reading and math scores rose to the level of "Excellent" in the state. And he ushered in new grants for community involvement, including preschool service expansion and development of afterschool and summer school programs to support his at-risk student population, which hovered at 75%. Tracy became a man with a mission and fire in his eye (T. Smith, personal communication, May 2014).

Our final story in this chapter is about Sandy Trach, a principal at Estabrook School in Lexington, MA. Sandy is a Blue Ribbon Principal recognized by the National Association of Elementary School Principals.

When we asked Sandy about her mindset and approach to education, she said, "I believe that 'all in' means *all in*! It's time for principals to listen loudly. There is too much jargon being used in education when talking to parents. There has to be a way to strip away the education speak and have authentic conversations."

Sandy believes educators are limited in having true impact on children if they don't know the parents.

Her school serves an urban community in Roxbury, MA. One Sunday she decided to attend the 12th Street Baptist Church, which is a historic political activist house of worship. Many of the parents of her students attend this church and, as you can imagine, when she walked into the church, all heads turned to notice the white woman coming into their sacred house of worship. WOW…she has a lot of nerve. Some of them had a wait-and-see attitude. What was her motive? Was she just checking off a to-do list item? What was her agenda?

Even though Sandy knew she would stick out like a sore thumb, she was still willing to take the risk of showing up. Her staff asked her *why*. Did she need someone to go with her? Was she going to be okay? On and on.

Nevertheless, because of the *weight* of her bedrock belief to empower the least, the last, and the often forgotten, she didn't just do it once but stayed consistent. She continued to attend the Sunday services at the 12th Street Baptist Church, and because of her consistency, the parents came to trust her and open up to her.

One of the core ways to connect with families is over a meal. As a result of showing up in this unexpected place, she was invited to break bread with these families in the fellowship hall after the church service. This allowed parents to get to know her and her to get to know them.

As Sandy got more comfortable talking to the community and trusting her intuition, she decided to stretch herself by taking on the hottest issues of the day and putting them on the table. As the conversations evolved, she encouraged parents to use a hashtag to openly share their ideas online.

It turns out there is a three-fold benefit to this approach. First of all, Sandy was able to talk to them about what is happening in real time about topics that are at the top of everyone's mind. That shows she is relevant and in touch with the times. Second, sharing the conversation through hashtags invites a wider audience to the virtual dinner table. They can post their feedback and share with other influencers. Finally, being totally transparent about the conversation builds trust, and that is the emotional glue of all relationships. Tapping into this parent voice is a powerful way to listen loudly.

Sandy told us that listening loudly is not a difficult concept to practice, but you do have to be disciplined in doing it. In other words, you can't do it just some of the time. People have to come to know you for doing it. She says that school settings tempt school officials and educators to be the ones to lead the agenda, the meetings, and the conversations. Instead, she advises leaders to let this notion go. She says, "Staff and parents know the children best, and I think it's our job as school leaders to set the conditions for listening to each other. So, my quest and challenge for all of us is how can we listen loudly—*together*?" (S. Trach, personal communication, February 25, 2016).

FROM OUR FLIGHT JOURNAL: ANTHONY SMITH, SUPERINTENDENT, DUVALL, WA

Developing Strength Through Difficulty

Here is a story about a leader whose difficult childhood lessons prepared him for his school leadership role. Dr. Anthony L. Smith is superintendent of Riverview School District in Duvall, WA. He attributes the district's success to the collaborative, committed culture that values students first in every decision that is made. Anthony Smith developed this perspective through the hard knocks of life.

When Anthony was an infant, his parents divorced and his mother remarried before Anthony was 2 years old. After that he had a fairly typical middle class life until he was 10. And then he says:

> *My dad committed suicide and my mom went to the bottom of a bottle of alcohol to self-medicate, which she was never able to escape. Boyfriends were in and out of the house, and I often became the defender for myself and my brothers against frequent emotional and sometimes physical abuse by them. I believe that it was this time period that impacted many of my values and beliefs.*

School became a refuge for him from an abusive home situation. Even though it was difficult sitting through classes at school with all the drama at home, he found teachers and mentors who taught him important life lessons.

- He discovered that to be the best leader, he had to listen more than he talked.
- He discovered that the team was only as good as the weakest in the group. So he constantly asked himself, "What can I do to build the capacity of others?"
- He learned to ask himself, "Are others better today because of what I did yesterday?"

Having to overcome more barriers than most, Anthony learned the resiliency to persevere when times got tough. He developed the grit to lead differently by *never* giving up on himself or others and to be relentlessly excited about striving for excellence (A. Smith, personal communication, November 24, 2015).

Research Background: Where's the Fuel?

What is required for our schools to truly break sound barriers in order to reach the promise of education for *every* student? School improvement efforts must tap into a framework that alters the system and culture of schools in fundamental ways. Marzano, Waters, and McNulty (2005) found that "deep change alters the system in fundamental ways, offering a dramatic shift in direction and requiring new ways of thinking and acting" (p. 66). Marzano et al. refer to this as "second-order change." Instead, though, most schools focus on doing incremental first-order changes that are short-lived with no lasting results.

Deep change causes a change in attitudes, values, and beliefs that drive a school and requires courage and effort. This is where continuous self-assessment is essential for school leaders.

The *Breaking Ranks®* (National Association of Secondary School Principals [NASSP], 2011) research showed that culture change starts with looking in the mirror—not only outside factors may be barriers; a leader's own practices and attitudes can hinder cultural shift. Creating conditions in which school improvement can grow is the first challenge of school improvement, and it starts with the principal's own thinking and interactions with people. Self-discovery grounds leadership and lets personal brilliance blossom.

What are your own values and beliefs? How does that play out in what you pay attention to in your work and the conversations you have with your staff? This forms your mindset, which creates the context for school culture even if you don't intend it.

In *Mindset: The New Psychology of Success*, Carol Dweck (2006) noted that what people believe about success drives their behavior. If educators don't really believe or expect that students can achieve at high levels, then school improvement efforts are doomed to failure. School leaders must do everything possible to help teachers attain a mindset that success is the result of time, work, and practice—not innate ability. That often means changing the culture of the school.

According to Seashore Louis and Wahlstrom (2011):

> Organizations with stronger cultures are more adaptable, have higher member motivation and commitment, are more cooperative

> and better able to resolve conflicts, have greater capacity for innovation and are more effective in achieving their goals (p. 52).

School leaders encourage these attributes when they set a tone supporting continual professional learning and engage teachers in conversations about their own growth.

Michael Fullan (2005) points to the critical role of the school's belief system for the sustainability of school improvement efforts:

> Sustainability is very much a matter of changes in culture: powerful strategies that enable people to question and alter certain values and beliefs as they create new forms of learning within and between schools, and across levels of the system. (p. 60)

The good news is that culture can be changed, and new beliefs and habits can be learned. Yet too often leaders want to point fingers at the things others are doing instead of focusing on themselves. It's easy to say, "If only so and so would do something differently—then everything would work well." But *you cannot change anybody else*. You only control yourself and how *you* respond in situations. And as a result, other people may decide to change *their responses to you* and to the system.

Leaders need to know their strengths so they can build upon them. But overreliance on one or two areas of strength can also become a weakness. Leaders need to know their challenge areas as well. This helps leaders manage areas of weakness through intentional development, while at the same time collaborating with others who have strengths in the needed areas. This ensures a proper balance of all the skills needed by the system to create great results.

And what happens if this self-discovery work is not done? *Breaking Ranks®* research says it can result in *unconscious incompetence*. It could mean "muddling along with a level of competence veiled in good intentions that does nothing to improve students learning within the schools" (NASSP, 2011).

You have to believe in people and have a sincere desire to move things forward. The demands on school leaders at all levels are daunting. Skills of leadership and communication are important to do the work. But if you are too busy to regularly undertake the reflection required to be effective in continuously developing yourself and others, then you are too busy to lead!

Call to Action: Envision Your Flight Plan

Now it is time for you to take some action. As a leader, change is a constant part of life. Carol Conklin-Spillane, Tracy Smith, and Sandy Trach all decided, in the words of Gandhi, to be the change they wanted to see in the world. Are you ready to do the same thing?

If so, stop trying to fly with the pack. You are called to go beyond where you are now, breaking sound barriers wherever you go.

In each chapter, we will be including two or three exercises to get you started reflecting upon and practicing the skills discussed in the chapter.

In this chapter, we want you to begin to feel the weight of your universal assignment and get very clear about your beliefs, purpose, and motivation. Do the exercises that follow to help you sum up the values, beliefs, and contributions you are meant to bring into the world. The exercises will help you envision a flight plan you could have for yourself.

Exercise 1.1: Mining Your Motivator

Every person is motivated by something in particular. When you know what motivates you, your role becomes more rewarding. You are driven by your passion, and you have a reason for getting out of bed in the morning. This kind of energy is natural and essential for personal success.

But sometimes you can lose sight of what gets you going and find yourself "in the rough." The following exercise will help you drill down on what your primary driver is. Knowing that, you are in a better position to ignite your own brilliance.

Part One

Ask yourself what kind of drivers, or payoffs, you seek in anything you do. For example, you may get a sense of satisfaction by making a difference, by helping people, or by overcoming barriers to meet a goal.

To get you thinking, review the list of payoffs, or motivators, on the following page, and **circle seven that speak to you** as the ones that impact you most.

Part Two

Review the seven choices you circled and **select the top three** that most motivate you, then record them in the space below.

____
____
____
____

Examine your top three motivators and **select the one** that you consider your Core Motivator. Record that in the space below.

____
____
____
____

Adapted from Cheryl Richardson (2005). *Stand Up for Your Life*.

(Continued)

(Exercise 1.1 Continued)

Communicate	Organize	Solve	Collaborate	Achieve
• Inspire	• Achieve	• Confidence	• Connect	• Cause
• Big Picture	• Assemble	• Be Aware	• Bond	• Empower
• Attract	• Accomplish	• Be Present	• Coach	• Increase
• Engage	• Build	• Mutual	• Comfort	• Direct
• Emphasize	• Opportunity	• Courage	• Run	• Excellence
• Reflect	• Ignite	• Impact	• Humor	• Distinguish
• Listen	• Develop	• Elegance	• Congruent	• Encourage
• Entertain	• Prioritize	• Mutual	• Energy	• Execute
• Enlighten	• Detail-Oriented	• Create	• Exhilaration	• Experiment
• Accurate	• Execute	• Awareness	• Unleash	• Risk
• Empathize	• Dedicate	• Honesty	• Honor	• Ethical
• Foster	• Invent	• Improve	• In Touch	• Influence
• Complete	• Master	• Understand	• Integrate	• Imagine
• Truthful	• Integrity	• Recognize	• Learn	• Add Value
• Master	• Relevant	• Earn the Right	• Mentor	• Purpose
• Explain	• Create	• Discover	• Assist	• Accept
• Tell a Story	• Lead	• New	• Experience	• Challenge
• Visionary	• Quest	• Opportunity	• Contribute	• Transform
• Leave a Legacy	• Multi-Task	• Adjust	• Appreciate	• Best Practice
		• Win-Win		• Make a Difference
		• Forward Momentum		

Adapted from Cheryl Richardson (2005), *Stand Up for Your Life*. New York, NY: Free Press.

Exercise 1.2: What Kind of Leader Do I Want to Be?

1.	• Why are you doing the work you've chosen to do? (What is your grand purpose?)	
2.	• What is the impact you want to have on your staff and your workplace environment?	
3.	• What concerns do you have when it comes to putting energy into leading a school improvement initiative?	
4.	• What would need to happen with this work for you to consider it a great success?	
5.	• What might stop you from attaining your goals?	
6.	• What is working really well for you right now regarding motivating and inspiring staff?	
7.	• How do you want to show up as the leader you want to be? (What characteristics do you want people to really "get" about you?)	

Exercise 1.3: Four Cornerstone Worksheet

Identify your four "cornerstones" (key characteristics) of great leadership. Then "unpack them" in detail below. Use a separate sheet for each cornerstone. This will help you know what specific skills, behaviors, and attitudes you want to develop.

Name of the Pillar	
Individual Level: How does this cornerstone look, sound, and feel as it is visible in me? What is its impact on me?	
In relationship(s): How does this cornerstone look, sound, and feel as it is visible in relationship with others? What is its impact on the relationship?	
In the broader community: How does this cornerstone look, sound, and feel when it is visible in the broader community? What is its impact on the community?	

Adapted from Jayne Warrilow (http://resonantcoaching.com/).

Visit www.releasingleadershipbrilliance.com to watch the Chapter 1 author video: "How You Can Leverage Weight to Enhance Your Personal Brilliance."

Collaborative Brilliance—Broadening the Vision Gives You "Lift"

Every Human Being Matters: Uproot Educational Apartheid

We believe that families in poor urban areas love their children as much as families in wealthy suburban areas. All these families believe that education is the path to a better life and prosperity for their children.

So as income disparity increases in the United States and around the world, we believe that enlightened educators are the *equalizers* that will give every child a lift no matter what the setting might be. We are called to end *educational apartheid,* which sociologist William Bielby says causes "unconscious bias" (Adler University, 2011). As a leader, you are challenged to be inclusive in your thinking every day, every way, everywhere. This is the urgent lift that is needed, not just in America but throughout the world.

In the United States, the Emancipation Proclamation of 1863 put an end to slavery on paper. However, more than 150 years later the psychological remnants of slavery have re-emerged in the form of #BlackLivesMatter. First of all, we believe that all lives matter. Simon knows that everyone who looks like him doesn't speak for him or think for him. However, as a black man in America, he understands the frustration of the #BlackLivesMatter movement despite not agreeing with some of their tactics. #BlackLivesMatter has emerged because of generational racism, police controversies, educational apartheid, and economic disparity. These factors have created hopelessness in pockets of the black community in America. Dale Bronner (2015), an influential black leader in Atlanta, says, "Hopeless people are hurtful people. But hopeful people are helpful people."

Arianna Huffington (2010) describes an economic hopelessness in her book, *Third World America: How Our Politicians Are Abandoning the Middle Class and Betraying the American Dream*:

> The warning lights on our national dashboard are flashing red: Our industrial base is vanishing, taking with it the kind of jobs that have formed the backbone of our economy for more than a century; our education system is in shambles, making it harder for tomorrow's workforce to acquire the information and training it needs to land good twenty-first-century jobs; our infrastructure—our roads, our bridges, our sewage and water, transportation, and electrical systems—is crumbling.
>
> And America's middle class, the driver of so much of our creative and economic success—the foundation of our democracy—is rapidly disappearing, taking with it a key component of the American Dream: the promise that, with hard work and discipline, our children will have the chance to do better than we did, just as we had the chance to do better than the generation before us.

Bold confidence in a better tomorrow empowers leaders to break their sound barriers and lift themselves and everyone else around them to heights unimaginable.

Educational leaders who create a lift raise the bar of expectations and refuse to settle for mediocrity. You have the ability to provide a lift by infusing teachers, students, and parents with hope. This hope in a better future equalizes education for everyone.

Michael Gerson (2015), in an editorial in the *Topeka Capital-Journal*, noted that the new education legislation, Every Student Succeeds Act (ESSA), "ends the backseat driving of the federal government in education policy. State and local officials will now be free to set academic goals and to determine whether schools are meeting them" (p. 4).

He says that for some states, this opens the doors for doing creative, positive new things for students. But there will be other states just doing the bare minimum because local politics and inertia prevent bold changes needed for disadvantaged students.

In Gerson's (2015) view, the group that loses in the Every Student Succeeds Act are disadvantaged students. He believes the achievement gaps between economic and racial groups is just going to continue to worsen.

Lift is going beyond the bare minimum to reach heights that are totally achievable if everyone is given a fair shot. We believe that a lift mindset breaks the sound barrier of educational apartheid that still exists in parts of the United States. Rather than being legislated systematically though, it is now subtle.

Simon explains it this way:

> *My kids attended a well-known elementary school in our small town of 2,500 residents in Orange County, Florida. It is a predominantly white school district, and many of the parents are key executives at several of the Fortune 500 companies. The school never has a money problem. Whatever the teachers need, the PTA makes it happen.*
>
> *I quickly learned that if Renee, the mother of my children, was not involved in PTA, we would be up a creek without a paddle in helping our children. I learned through Renee that there seemed to be an unofficial, unsanctioned, undocumented maneuvering of kids to certain teachers from grade to grade. So she had to build alliances with other influential mothers who had the ear of the principal, knew the best teachers by subject, and wrote a check from time to time for various fundraisers.*
>
> *I noticed that if our daughter and son didn't have a peer buddy in the classroom (a relationship that was often intentionally orchestrated by a helicopter parent), they were fresh out of luck. As our kids moved from elementary to middle school, it was the same mindset. There was a mad dash to make sure that kids got the best teacher and classes. Parents who were new to the area and didn't know the game were left out in the cold.*

Simon's story is uncomfortable and not easy to digest. But in our gut, we know it is often true. While in the affluent area of town you might find helicopter parents, in an inner city you will likely discover that many disadvantaged students whose families are living at or below the poverty line have a different experience of school (Singleton, 2015). Expectations are often higher in the wealthy school district and lower in the poor school district. This is as much of a "haves versus have nots" issue as it is a racial issue.

We believe one of the ways to equalize education that provides a lift is to "hug children with your words." It may sound simplistic, but it is powerful in execution.

Your words matter. Language is the software of the mind. Every word you say creates an outcome. Choose your words wisely because they carry power. Love and respect have no color. Every day educators have the ability to use their words to say, "I love you and I believe in you" by how they think about and treat students.

Peter Drucker (1995), management guru, once said that leadership is not "magnetic personality." It is not "making friends and influencing people." Leadership is lifting a person's vision to higher sights, raising a person's performance to a higher standard, the building of a personality beyond normal limitations.

Leaders Create Relationships That Lift

Lift has generational implications. Thirteen years of K-12 shapes a mindset with an impact that is felt 100 years down the road. If *Weight*

is about creating a culture, then *Lift* is about offering all students a hand up, *not* a handout.

When people experience a lift in their education, it helps them to another rung on the ladder of progress that pulls another generation forward. As one hand reaches for the next rung of the ladder, there is someone at the top pulling them up instead of pushing them down. Leaders who operate with lift thinking come from a place of abundance instead of scarcity. With abundance thinking, they are not worried about withholding information from others. Instead, as Liz Wiseman (2010) suggests in her book, *Multipliers: How the Best Leaders Make Everyone Smarter*, these kinds of leaders freely share with others everything they need to know to be successful because by doing so, they are making room to grow within themselves as well.

When leaders come from a place of scarcity, they fear that if someone else knows something they don't, that other person will get ahead of them. What they don't understand is that the entire world is constantly shifting around them, and if they aren't helping to lift others up, they won't be able to soar either. Leaders in various fields and industries are now using their influence to create a lift in education despite the complexity of a century-old legacy system. If Uber can disrupt the taxi cab industry in less than five years, and Airbnb can surpass other hotel chains in revenue with just a tenth of employees, what do you think can happen in education? Salim Ismail, in his book *Exponential Organizations: Why New Organizations Are Ten Times Better, Faster, and Cheaper Than Yours,* says, "some organizations come to rely on a paradigm that performed perfectly up until the moment it didn't, and that is suddenly, often inexplicably, out of date" (Ismail, Malone, & van Geest, 2014).

Two examples of attempts at educational innovation from noneducators are Lauren Jobs (widow of Steve Jobs) and Larry Ellison. Lauren Jobs has donated up to $50 million to launch XQ: The Super School Project, which is to redesign the high school experience from scratch for American teenagers.

And Larry Ellison, founder of Oracle, is building a 64,000-square-foot high school that will house 550 students and 30 teachers next to Oracle's Silicon Valley, California, headquarters. It will be called Design Tech High School and will focus on teaching science, technology engineering, problem solving, and design thinking to prepare students for careers in technology (Liedtke, 2015). These innovative schools demonstrate the Greek proverb that says a society grows great when old men plant trees whose shade they know they shall never sit in. It shows hope for the future.

Innovative Partnerships as a Leadership Edge

But you don't need to create a new school to be an innovative leader. There are countless examples of everyday leaders like yourself who've decided to take steps to transform education from the inside. For instance, in the *Breaking Ranks®* research (NASSP, 2001), Breakthrough Schools found that collaboration within grade levels, across grade levels, and across schools provided the backbone of sustainability for school improvement changes. Successful transformation and improved student achievement depends on collaboration. The old paradigm of top-down, organizational-chart leadership was good for sorting but too restrictive and bureaucratic to meet student needs. It was good for organizing but bad at customizing and adjusting for individual learning.

Here are examples of award-winning principals who have provided significant lift for their students by partnering with their communities in creative ways.

Sheila Harrity, Principal, Worcester Technical High School (NASSP 2011 Breakthrough School)

Worcester, MA

Sheila Harrity is an example of a leader who became the lift she wanted to see in her community. She is a New England educated, white, suburban woman who drives a Volvo, and she had a bodacious vision for this urban school where students come from the projects, travel to school by public transportation, and have a generational legacy of poverty. Sheila Harrity has no fear. She learned how to raise money in the trenches to fulfill the dream of lifting kids out of poverty through education. Simon first met Sheila when they did an interview on SchoolTube.com during an NASSP annual conference. He wanted to find out what she had done to release brilliance at Worcester Technical High School. He was blown away.

When Sheila took over as principal of the school, it was the lowest-performing high school in the city and one of the poorest performing vocational schools in the state. One of the disparities that infuriated her the most was that expectations and rigor in her urban school did not match the higher standards of the suburban schools. She resolved to raise the bar of expectation to the level of expectations in the suburban schools where she had previously taught. She implemented honors courses and joined AVID (Advancement Via Individual Determination) so that she could tap into local resources and find tutors willing to come to the school to help students. She wrote a state grant to offer Advanced Placement courses.

But there was pushback by some not willing to offer this type of rigor in a vocational school. Sheila believed that in order to give students a lift in life, they needed to be supported by having strong rigor and high expectations in their classes so that they could meet the changing expectations of business and industry after graduation. She and her teachers made it a priority to connect students with real-world examples. Previously, students came to school feeling like they just had to memorize and regurgitate irrelevant information for a test and then they could forget it. But in this vocational setting, the question about why-I-should-learn-this was being answered as the students put a robot together in tech ed class, worked with various mathematical equations in culinary class to determine amounts of ingredients to use in a recipe, or learned the chemistry of how dyes and chemicals work in cosmetology. Sheila said that her mindset is "we-focused" instead of "me-focused." She pulled together a team of administrators and department heads—35 people in all. She said they created "our goals" not "my goals." Everyone was held accountable for results.

Their state test scores started going up, the graduation rate was increasing, and the dropout rate was going down. Pride was rising, but they didn't stop there. The staff realized that they needed to kick it into a higher gear. Sheila and her team noticed that two weeks before students would sit for the AP Exam, state exam, or make a career decision, they would begin to sabotage themselves because they lacked the self-confidence to make it to the graduation finish line. Many students just weren't used to being successful. She and her administrative team decided that they needed a motivational coach or person who could give the kids a pre-exam talk similar to a pre-game talk before players enter the field. Once again, Sheila talked up this idea to visitors to the school, and sure enough, a donor stepped up to underwrite this motivational experience.

Two weeks prior to exam time, Worcester Technical High School put 1,400 students and 150 staff members on 44 buses and rented out the Hanover Theater in Worcester. Most people thought that Sheila and her core team were crazy for letting 1,400 kids loose in the city. But the students didn't "disappear" downtown. Sheila believed that kids rise to the occasion based on the expectation—and all of them did! They listened to Liz Murray, whose life story became a TV film, *Homeless to Harvard*. She shared with the students how she overcame obstacles and succeeded. The following day the students were already asking who Sheila would bring as speaker for the next year. The boost was a success, and the same donor who said yes the first time has not stopped saying yes for the last seven years.

As Sheila works with the community, she continually asks herself, "How do we align the partnerships in the community to impact the workforce pipeline and have an impact in North Central Massachusetts?" She is strengthening business partnerships by having a full-service bank connect to their business tech program. Now students can do a co-op program with bank tellers at 17 area banks. And her newest vision is to develop a 7,500-square-foot veterinarian clinic that will serve the area. She has already raised the $2 million to do it and built in six college credits for students to work alongside a veterinarian from Becker College.

Sheila is now superintendent of Massachusetts Regional Vocational Technical School, which serves 18 communities, two cities, and 16 towns all the way up to the New Hampshire border. She realizes that all of this personal and student success simply started with a group of individuals who came together and decided what was best for kids (S. Harrity, personal communication, November 23, 2015).

FROM OUR FLIGHT JOURNAL: JOE NELSON, MIDDLE SCHOOL PRINCIPAL, PASS CHRISTIAN, MS

Inspiration From Disaster

Sound barriers sometimes arise from natural disasters. Joe Nelson is the principal of Pass Christian Middle School in Pass Christian, MS. He was there in 2005 when Hurricane Katrina hit. Their town was ground zero for some of the worst devastation. Ninety percent of the families at the school lost their homes. The property tax base was completely wiped out. Everything was destroyed!

But Joe did not use this excuse for losing focus on student learning. He set up office in the trunk of his car. He rallied staff and community to access mobile classrooms with FEMA money. Once classrooms were in place, he brought staff back together and held them and the students to the same high learning standards as before. Hurricane Katrina was not going to be a reason for students to slide by at his school!

The level of student achievement began to steadily rise and continued for six successive years. They earned Blue Ribbon status in 2012. And his school continues to be among the top-rated middle schools in his state. Joe and his faculty are a model of how to turn the sound barriers brought on by a catastrophe into a story of renewed hope and rebirth using grit and resilience (J. Nelson, personal communication, December 3, 2015).

Todd Nesloney, Principal, Webb Elementary (NAESP National Distinguished Principal)

Navasota, TX

Another example of an award-winning school that has mobilized the community to provide lift for its children is Webb Elementary in Navasota, Texas. The elementary school in rural south Texas serves 750 students. Principal Todd Nesloney and his staff wanted to get the community more involved. But they were not having any success with traditional strategies for getting parents involved. As an innovative leader, Todd told his staff they needed to stop trying to get the parents *in* the school. Instead, they needed to find ways to *take the school to the parents*—and to the community and local churches—in order to build relationship capital within the community.

Todd and his teachers decided to go to an apartment complex where the majority of students lived. To blend in better with the families and to appear more accessible, they wore shorts, T-shirts, and flip-flops. They brought barbecue grills, fired them up, and began cooking hot dogs for any resident who showed up. They partnered with students from the high school and that night cooked 350 hot dogs for the families in the complex. When parents asked why they were doing this, Todd told them, "Because we love you and care about you."

Just imagine the power of this action! What an incredible way to extend an olive branch before it's even necessary or required. It creates conditions for conversation and listening. Todd adamantly stated that they went to serve parents with no agenda, not asking them to do homework or prod their children to read for 20 minutes a night. His approach was to let the families see that staff care about them and their kids. More important, he believed that it was important for the teachers to connect with parents and students outside the walls of the school. The barbecue is now a tradition that occurs several times a year.

As a result of this community connection, Todd now has a venue for his staff to gain a sense of context regarding the lifestyle and environment the students come from. He says that poverty is generally understood in three ways by teachers: They've heard about it, seen it, or lived it. Teachers who haven't come from poverty don't understand what students are going through. After an event like this, they can now empathize with kids because they see what is happening in real time in their homes.

Visiting students on their own turf is eye-opening for many teachers. The kids invite them into their home or apartment because they are not embarrassed about where they live. They are not concerned about not having a bed to sleep in when there are seven people living in a one-bedroom apartment. When teachers have a glimpse, they can better understand why homework is not turned in or why a student may show up angry. It gives teachers the reason *why* they need to be creative in designing the homework practice they assign.

Todd has also invited businesses to get involved with the school. One summer the school was being remodeled, and they desperately needed some things that were outside of the construction contract. The school handed out more than 300 fliers to local business people, inviting them to come to an open house. Todd took these business professionals through the remodeling area and did a little vision casting. His fundamental belief was that provision follows vision.

The business community attendees were a little apprehensive at first because they thought that he was going to ask them for a financial investment. Instead, he said, "We don't know what you bring to the table." He simply asked, "How would you like to get involved?"

One business donated designers to build office chairs for some classrooms. Others donated workers to help move furniture and finish some of the general maintenance tasks that had been put aside because of the remodeling and now had to get done before school started. By leveraging relationship capital and doing "friend-raising" instead of fundraising, Todd's school was ready and beautiful for the students on the first day back!

Another radical approach to creating a lift in the community focused on trying to reach the men involved in students' lives. The first attempt was a Watch Dog event, but only two men showed up. Todd's team then decided to create a dinner to "Celebrate the Gentlemen" of the community. It's important to understand that in the community where he was principal, 40% to 60% of students don't have a father in their lives because he is either incarcerated, absent, or the student is living in a Child Protective Services family placement. The school was only expecting (hoping for!) about 125 men to come. But amazingly they had to cut the RSVPs off at 640!

The Celebrate the Gentlemen event ended up hosting 600 men from the community. The school partnered with the VFW, city hall, and the school's district office to help get all the tables, chairs, and supplies they needed to pull it off.

They invited three speakers from the local community who represented the local ethnic breakdown. And they held a panel at which students spoke about why the men present were important in their lives. Everyone got a book because it enabled the men to continue their relationship with the student. Even if they could not read it themselves, they could use it to interact with their student.

Todd later reflected about the evening's success:

> *Fathers don't come to reading night or family game night or donuts for Dads, but for some reason they came to this one night. I believe it's because men are sick and tired of being told what they are not doing. As a man, I can clearly relate that men want to be recognized for what they are doing right instead of what they are doing wrong.*

Todd went on to say that one father was so impacted by this experience that he made an arrangement with his employer to volunteer time every Wednesday at the school. As a result of his commitment, the school adopted him as the "School Dad" (T. Nesloney, personal communication, July 7, 2016).

Todd has proven himself to be an exceptional leader by trying unconventional approaches to collaborate with the community for the sake of his students. He created micro-moments with his staff by bringing them into the lives of the students. These micro-moments enable them to be supportive and creative about homework completion because they understand the child may have significant challenges in his or her home living arrangements. Another micro-moment happens when local businesspeople contribute their expertise and time as volunteers, sharing their belief in the power of relationships and the importance of mentoring. Most important, he found a way to celebrate what families were doing right by honoring the fact that even children being raised without a father still have important men in their lives who can serve as mentors and provide emotional support. Each of these efforts showed Todd's commitment to providing lift for others.

Mark Shanoff, Principal, Ocoee Middle School (NAESP National Distinguished Principal)

Ocoee, FL

Mark Shanoff, NAESP National Distinguished Principal at Ocoee Middle School in Ocoee, FL, asks business leaders to engage in the school improvement process by reminding them that once these students graduate from high school or college, they will become part of the local workforce.

Mark especially targets small-business leaders. He tells them, "Our students will become your economic drivers." He has developed a dynamic partnership with these business leaders that gives the school a strategic perspective. The partnership group identifies skills that students need to learn for the workforce, and it opens up opportunities for students to connect what they are learning to real-world experiences. Businesses see this partnership as a viable reason to be involved with schools.

For example, the city of Winter Garden, Florida, is a small municipality. They don't control the school but are very active in Ocoee Middle School where Mark is principal. Generations are represented in this town because many of the people here don't move far away from where they were born. The municipality also has a segment of the population that is living in generational poverty, and for many of them there has been no way out of poverty. Connecting with the local businesses makes sense as a strategy to break the cycle of poverty by providing students the real-life skills they will need to be gainfully employed after graduation.

The wife of the mayor of Winter Garden was a third-grade teacher at Mark's school. Using that network connection, Mark invited the mayor to come to school to work as a classroom volunteer on a regular basis. Soon the school started seeing more city employees coming to the school to volunteer in the classroom, repair something, or participate in Teach-In or Career Day.

Mark realized that this was an opportunity to strengthen a relationship with the city that also could stretch to opportunities for students. He asked the mayor what workforce skills were most needed by the city. The mayor named things like utility workers, city planners, truckers, finance workers, firefighters, and police officers.

Mark didn't stop there. He then asked if the mayor could place advanced math students with the city planning folks to help that department collect some data. Soon students were working on stoplight and speed bump studies. These types of experiences really helped students connect the dots between what they were learning in the classroom and what they were seeing in the real world.

The students shared the information they collected with the city workers. Relationships bloomed as students grew in confidence, learning that they could become useful information resources for city issues. And city workers came to know and appreciate the skills and ingenuity of young people in their city. By partnering with the community in this way, the school provides a way out of poverty for the students while allowing them to remain in the community with their families.

Finally, Mark likes to invite legislators to come to his school. They most often see a completely different learning experience than they had in their own schooling. They expect to see things through a certain lens, but they find out that schools are much different than even just a few years ago. Mark believes that the more politicians are invited into the school system, the more educators can influence them to think like entrepreneurs. Educators can help them realize that schools are the seed ground for workforce and job creators. Funding education and ensuring quality resources for *all* students is an important investment in the future (M. Shanoff, personal communication, July 7, 2016).

Sheila Harrity, Todd Nesloney, and Mark Shanoff have dared to dream big and mobilized their communities to *be a lift* for students. They have energized their communities even when the communities didn't understand how important their role was. Engaging and inspiring the community is a very important aspect for providing lift, especially in high poverty areas where parents sometimes have to learn unwritten rules of advocacy and don't have the luxury of time and resources to personally engage because they are working more than one job to make ends meet.

Research Background: Where's the Fuel?

We need not only individual parents but also whole communities to provide lift for *all* children. But finding consensus within the community and harnessing its energy are not easy tasks. Such work creates opportunities for participation by all stakeholders in creating a plan. And it is very hard to oppose change if stakeholders see the data and understand the benefits for students. It is not lack of effort that most often kills reforms. It is a failure to address the process of culture building. And shared leadership, no matter the form (leadership teams, professional learning communities, parent advisory groups), has a profound and lasting impact on the culture of school (Mero & Hartzman, 2012).

James Rourke and Elizabeth Boone (2012) add that all of the Breakthrough Schools have been successful largely because of the collaborative way they have organized to work as professionals. They worked together toward a common goal, and all of the planning, decision making, and problem solving emerged through teamwork.

The Power of Involving Parents and Community

Belief in this power of collaboration is the heart of both personal development and school success. It shows the importance of developing meaningful relationships with staff, students, parents, and community. These relationships foster mutual goals and trust and create strong learning environments for students.

FROM OUR FLIGHT JOURNAL: TIFFANY ANDERSON, FORMER SUPERINTENDENT, JENNINGS, MO

Connecting With the Community

While Dr. Tiffany Anderson was superintendent in the Jennings School District, just outside of St. Louis, MO, she made a huge positive impact on the system. Jennings is a predominantly poor community, mostly African American, which underwent a tremendous academic overhaul in just four years under Anderson's guidance. In 2015, after three years with the district, 93% of the students graduated in four years, and 100% of those graduates were going on to post-secondary education or a job. When asked about this turnaround, she said, "Everybody can do something when you figure out what the needs are." In Jennings, the schools not only provided academics; they became the heart of the community.

She opened dialogue with local churches, civic agencies, and businesses and asked, "How can we collaborate? What can we do to serve kids better in our community?" Through those conversations she found out that food was a problem for families. So she set up food pantries in the schools, giving away more than 8,000 pounds of food to 200 to 400 families every month.

She worked with nearby Washington University to provide a pediatrician and health clinics in schools so that children's health needs were met. And she invited families to use the school laundry facilities during off hours for free, in exchange for one hour of volunteer time at the school.

Tiffany also made talking to students a priority—students who were at the top of the honor roll as well as those at the bottom, and even those who had dropped out. She asked, "What is your experience of our schools? What have you done and accomplished? What would have helped you even more?" Through those conversations, she helped administrators and teachers see school through the students' eyes.

Her focus on conversations was not a marketing gimmick merely to promote good will. She was about organizing the community to come together to serve student needs. Tiffany was adamant that the quality of a child's education should not be determined by a child's ZIP code (T. Anderson, personal communication, July 20, 2016).

Collaborating across schools and communities is never an easy task. There are many common barriers that can get in the way of building consensus and involving broad stakeholder participation. Marceta became superintendent of a school district that had just been through a series of painful, defeated bond issue elections that had splintered the community into warring factions. Trust and morale within the school system were at the lowest point possible. Teachers and school administrators were feeling beaten down because of lack of support for badly needed school improvements. And community members in the two rural towns and Native American reservation served by the district were frustrated because they felt no one was listening to their perspective.

Marceta explains:

> *This was the mess I walked into when I became superintendent of the district. Just prior to my arriving, the school board had boldly forced consolidation of two K–8 buildings, one in each town, to form a K–4 center at one site and a 5–8 center at the other. And they were determined to proceed with another bond issue election. It failed by one vote, which was closer than any election in the past. This encouraged them to try one more time, and that election failed in a tie vote.*

The school board finally gave up on the bond issue elections. The grade configurations were changed, but the structures still needed major renovations and upgrading. The task was rebuilding trust and relationships. What did the people want for the children in these communities? Each person Marceta and board members talked to had slightly different and legitimate viewpoints. How do you find out where some consensus could be built? Public forums only seemed to bring out the voice of factions and didn't allow for thoughtful consideration of multiple perspectives. What was needed was a *conversation process* that brought people together in a public way to build understanding and consensus. That is when Marceta read about the Community Conversation model for public engagement developed by Public Agenda. She contacted them and, after more investigation, asked them to help the district host a Community Conversation around this issue: What should be the priority of education for the children in our school district?

The leadership team that came together to plan the event involved broad sectors of the community. It was an *invited, facilitated* conversation—not just a drop-in, come-if-you-have-an-ax-to-grind forum. They wanted the typical influencers to attend but also the invisible, the voiceless, and the argumentative factions of the community. How else were they going to build true consensus unless they had *all* the voices in the room? They planned food and babysitting, issued invitations, phoned people to encourage their attendance, and tracked lists of people who registered to come. Then they organized the attendees into heterogeneous small discussion groups to ensure variety in age, gender, position, economic status, and life experiences.

From among the planners they selected and trained individuals to be facilitators of each of the small conversation groups. Their role was to initiate the core question themes, ensure that each voice was heard, and move the conversation along.

The four-hour event occurred on a Saturday morning. More than 100 people participated. The teacher voice was present in each conversation group, but school administrators and board members were present only as observers. Their role was to *listen with an open mind* to what they heard in the conversations. The results were amazing! At the final wrap-up session, as groups reported out their key ideas—both points of consensus and places of disagreement—themes actually emerged across groups. This gathering of people representing all sectors, age groups, and economic levels within the community clearly pointed to a priority purpose. And it wasn't to learn basic skills or to get a good job (both of which the administrative team predicted would likely be the priority purposes). No. Their message was that they wanted education to help their children become *well-rounded individuals*.

That really changed the perspective of the school leaders. The community didn't want just a "basic education" (reading, writing, and arithmetic), nor did they want education just focused on job training. They wanted their children to have a *broad* education. They said, "If our kids are well-educated, they can go anywhere and do anything they want. It's not just about having a job. It's about having opportunities in life."

That conversation changed everything. Bridges started to be built across factions. Conversations about school facility needs began to focus on the instructional and library additions in the planning rather than the athletic and public area improvements. There had always been both in the design plans, but school leadership had incorrectly thought the community would be more interested in the athletic/public improvements than the classroom ones. And then community organizations and agencies began to step up to the plate. They began to see possibilities and points of connection to the school. But then another sound barrier raised its ugly head. That is the sound barrier of hiding behind The Budget.

Time and again, Marceta has seen that money is often a sound barrier that emerges when educators begin to dream bigger and want to provide lift for their students. Educators limit themselves from moving forward because "we just don't have any money." They seem to say, "We are poor, after all. Just look at our neighborhood."

She has seen it time and again:

- The agriculture teacher who never invested in planning an expansion for his course offerings because "he knew there wouldn't be any money to fund it."
- The principal who wanted an additional staff person devoted to keeping middle schoolers caught up on their homework assignments, but he never really expected it to happen.
- The school board who gave up on ever trying to improve high school library facilities because "the community would never allow the tax increase necessary to pay for the remodeling."

Do you see the pattern here? In each case, educators dreamed about good ideas but gave up without trying because "there is no money anyway." The budget becomes a huge barrier. Educators often hear, "No. Sorry. Can't fund that. It's not in the budget." But the thing is, maybe it *could* be. How do you expand that budget? How do you leverage the money that *is* available? One way is to look for outside funding sources—grants or seed money contributions from local businesses. Another way is to build coalitions with other like-minded community groups and organizations by creating a meaningful vision of what *could be* if we worked together.

Marceta talks about her experience:

> *I was superintendent during a period of very tight budget constraints. One of the important programs we had to cut was summer school. But our administrative team talked frequently about the value and need of summer support, especially for our at-risk*

> *students. So I began to start conversation with leaders in other youth-serving organizations and agencies—social services, local health department, juvenile justice system, sheriff's office, extension agency, local Tribal Council.*

These conversations about their mutual interests led to a county-wide meeting to discuss how they might work together for the benefit of youth. Each agency had small amounts of money earmarked for youth programs, and each group had a further network of community resources they could tap into (city library, the Boys' and Girls' Club, 4-H programs, idle school buses for transportation). Together, they formed a coalition, with each agency contributing financial or in-kind support to fund a six-week summer enrichment program to keep kids learning through the summer. Marceta recalls:

> *It was kind of like the loaves and fishes biblical story. Everybody contributed a little bit and together they designed a really beneficial program targeting our most vulnerable children. It wasn't just a school program; it was a community commitment!*

This coalition has stayed together for more than 10 years now. It is built on relationships and a common vision of working together to provide important opportunities for children. Many of the original adults in the group have transitioned out over the years, but new ones have stepped up to take their places and new groups and agencies have joined.

It's not easy to keep coalitions together and running smoothly, but the energy put into doing the work is worth it! It leverages small pots of money that civic institutions have for special programs, and it engages the hearts of individuals around meaningful, mutual goals.

Call to Action: File Your Flight Plan

Complete one or more of the following exercises to help you consider how to move your school in this direction of *community support and engagement*. The first one provides you with a discussion guide to deepen your understanding and relationship as partners.

Exercise 2.1: "SPARK" Innovation in Your Partnerships

The underlying purpose of building a partnership with the community is to create, shape, and expand the educational experience and impact for students. Innovation-driven partnerships attract and engage people, working together for success of *all* students.

Here are five key question areas your partnership can use to help you focus on your strengths, work collaboratively, and create innovative experiences for students.

S	What is the *synergy* in the partnership that draws you to work for children? The first thing you want to discuss is how you and your partner(s) find meaning in connecting around creating remarkable experiences for students. Briefly remind yourselves that you are in this together. What is each partner's critical role in serving others? How can you leverage this natural synergy?
P	How can we best contribute toward each other's *purpose*? Once you understand where you and your partners synergize, this question lets you and your partner identify expectations and roles. By listening to your partner's responses, you can understand each other's purpose in the student experience. Then clarify and manage how you can help meet each other's objectives. Determine ways in which you can innovate to move beyond today's current situation.
A	What are we hoping to *accomplish*? When you ask this, you and your partner(s) are trying to find out what things are important to each of you and what you are both hoping to accomplish in the way of innovation. Be prepared to ask further questions and clarify each other's understanding so you can know on a deeper level what each of you really needs. As a result, you and your partner(s) will know what is important and what to focus on.
R	What does the ideal *relationship* look like? This question allows you and your partner(s) to describe the kind of working relationship you want to have. Here are some follow-up questions that can help you: How often should we meet? What is the best way for us to communicate? How do we keep the new ideas flowing? Who else should be involved?

K	How can we *keep* the relationship positive and "for life?" On an ongoing basis, it is a good idea for you to exchange feedback with your partner(s). When you ask this question regularly, you show your partner(s) that you care about their opinions and that you are constantly striving for improvement. Keep each other motivated to continue raising the bar by trying new ideas.

Exercise 2.2: Action Planning for Partners

Use this exercise to help you plan your work together as partners. It makes the work explicit, identifies the key partners needed, and clarifies the greater goal(s) everyone wants.

Use each row to identify the key work for each partner and then use the tool again to plan specific tasks in the partner project.

Example: Summer School Planning

Partner	Share What?	With Whom?	How?	When?	Desired Outcomes?
Sheriff's office	SRO officers	Summer school staff	Provide classes in bicycle and street safety	Two weeks during summer session	Building relationships with local law enforcement
Tribal Council	Swimming pool at Boys'/Girls' Club • Free entrance fee • Lifeguard	Summer school staff	Provide free daily entry for groups of summer school students	Different groups each day during summer school	Every summer school child gets swim time at least once per week during the program

(Continued)

Exercise 2.2: (Continued)

Extension office	Home Econo-mist staff person	Summer school staff	Offer classes in child-care safety and cooking	Two weeks during summer session	Teach self-care and family-support skills to children

Exercise 2.3: Public Agenda Community Conversation Project

Visit the Public Agenda website here: www.publicagenda.org/pages/choicework-homepage

There are many resources available on this website to help you open up conversations and discussions about topics important to your parents and community members. Under the tab "Our Library," many discussion topics are listed for community conversations. I expanded the K–12 section on the discussion starters webpage and found 19 issues. Below are 3 examples of the 19 offered by Public Agenda:

- How can we ensure that all children have excellent teachers?
- Creating a formula for success in low-performing schools
- Ready for 21st-century careers

Each discussion starter has three or four typical responses and asks participants to discuss each, weighing the pros and cons for the community. The different perspectives are drawn from what the public thinks about an issue, based on surveys and focus groups, as well as what experts and leaders say about it in policy debates. They are not meant to be definitive but to get the conversation started based on several legitimate perspectives. Such conversations are frequently a solid first step toward new partnerships and initiatives.

Public Agenda's model for Community Conversations encompasses several key principles:

- **Local Nonpartisan Sponsoring Coalition:** A coalition of local organizations and institutions to sponsor and help organize the Community Conversation.
- **Diverse Participants:** Participation that represents a cross-section of the community—not just the usual suspects—to ensure that all groups and stakeholders are represented and heard from.
- **Dialogue in Small, Diverse Groups:** Small group discussions facilitated by trained and objective moderators and recorders who document the proceedings for effective follow-up.

Rather than lectures by experts, or gripe sessions by angry constituents, well-designed Community Conversations create a frank, productive problem-solving process in which diverse ideas are put on the table, diverse participants sit at the table, and people work to find common ground and solutions.

Visit www.releasingleadershipbrilliance.com to watch the Chapter 2 author video: "How You Can Create Relationships That Lift."

Team Brilliance—Building Capacity to Collaborate Gives You "Thrust"

Collaboration: The Emotional Glue for School Culture

When educators get together, the topic often turns to teams. Jennifer Abrams pinpoints the problem well: "We do not prepare our educators for the collaborative skills and mindset to be effective in teamwork. We give them a credential to teach students, but not how to talk to adults" (J. Abrams, personal communication, February 17, 2016).

Simon tells this story about his experience as new leader of a team:

> *When I first got promoted to Sales Director and New Business Development Director of Disney Institute, I thought that I was hot stuff. The reality was I was clueless. But I didn't want anyone to know that I didn't know what the heck I was doing. My positive attitude was a mile wide, but my knowledge of how to do the job was an inch deep. Sadly, my team around me really wanted to help me. But my ego edged greatness out and wouldn't let me ask for help.*
>
> *My leader at the time was Larry Lynch, who could double as a twin of then-CEO of the Walt Disney Company, Michael Eisner. He could see I was losing leadership altitude very quickly. He had my previous role and knew the stresses, challenges, and*

pressure of managing the profit and loss of a burgeoning start-up entity.

The team members were committed to the cause and wanted to see me succeed. However, I was blinded in thinking that I was an Affirmative Action promotion and that every person who didn't look like me or wasn't from my ZIP code was against me. I felt like I had to prove a point. I had to change their perception of black men in America, where the media has portrayed most black men as being incarcerated; on drugs; only capable of running, catching, and throwing a ball; and having the ability to make a baby but never possessing the capacity to be a father.

As the first African-American Sales Director of Disney Institute, I felt the weight of my slave ancestors, the dream of Dr. Martin Luther King, the conviction of Malcom X, the courage of Rosa Parks, and the fight for corporate equality of the Rev. Jesse Jackson on my shoulders. This created a sound barrier within me that prevented me from seeking help. I didn't know how to be a team player let alone lead the team.

Eventually, human resources and organizational development were called in to do an intervention. They took me through the tried-and-true human resources process called Start–Stop–Continue. Would you believe that I still have a copy of it almost 20 years later?

Here is the bottom line: I was, at best, a boss with an agenda instead of a leader with a vision. I communicated to the team via e-mail but never really connected to the team even when I was face to face. There was always an arm's-length relationship because I didn't want to get close to them. I didn't want them in my business and I didn't want to know what they did over the weekend or stick my nose in their business.

My attitude at that time before I had a radical transformation was simple. I don't care what the name of your dog, cat, son, daughter, niece, or nephew is. You have a job and now go forth and create magic.

Well, my boss called me into his office and it was not a very pixie-dusted conversation. He asked me to walk through a typical day when I came in the office. I said that I like to read my e-mails, return my calls, and then run off to a meeting to rub shoulders with the senior brass and kiss up to those who could promote me.

Without missing a beat, he said that would be your problem right there. I said no way. Yet he saw that I managed the vertical relationships really well but was challenged when it came to horizontal relationships.

For the next 18 months, I had to go to Disney University once a month for two hours to really understand what it meant to be a leader. The one thing that really stays with me even to this day is a quote from John Maxwell: "People don't care how much you know until they know how much you care." My team felt that I treated them like social security numbers in the HR payroll system instead of vibrant human beings who could make a significant contribution to the future of the organization.

Well, after 18 months I had made a radical transformation. I think it partially had to do with the awareness that if I didn't break my need to be right, Disney was going to invite me to find my happiness elsewhere. My strategy of leading had to change, and it did, thank goodness! I became emotionally connected when I made it about them instead of me.

In Simon's story, each person on the team had something brilliant to share. But he was blocking it from happening by not creating an environment of mutual caring and safety that would allow their *collective* brilliance to rise.

Marceta has seen that same effect in some of the schools in which she works. These schools seem to have a pervasive culture of isolating the work. People mostly work alone. They interact with colleagues but not often about instruction or supporting students. They don't depend upon colleagues to help them learn new things. And they don't feel a responsibility to help others grow professionally. That's someone else's role in the system (an instructional coach, a team leader or departmental chair, a district staff developer, a principal).

Yet C.R. Leana, in her 2011 research, studied the effect of "social capital." Social capital is the collaborative power of a group (teamwork). Her findings were astonishing!

- Social capital (effective collaborative teams) is highly correlated to positive student achievement outcomes.
- When high social capital is present with strong human capital (talented individuals), schools do even better.
- Teachers with low human capital working in the schools with high social capital get better outcomes than those in schools with lower social capital.

Teamwork Creates Thrust

It seems that being in a school around others who are working effectively as teams rubs off on teachers! But problems with dysfunctional teams is a persistent topic of many conversations among Marceta's clients and in the educational communities with which she works.

What does teamwork have to do with *Thrust,* the third force of flight? While *Lift* pulls people up, *Thrust* helps them move forward. Leana's research on social capital clearly showed that when teachers work effectively in teams, it raises the level of professionalism and achievement in a school. Effective teams move the work forward in a positive direction. Teaming creates the kind of thrust that helps develop professional presence within individuals and schools.

Simon has a cousin, Maia Stephen, who exhibits high professional presence. She is a second-grade teacher in a school in Northwest Detroit. It's a Title I school and she has been teaching there for 18 years.

For readers who live outside the United States, Title I schools receive additional funding to bridge the achievement gap between low-income students and other students. Title I schools must have at least 40% of the students receiving free or reduced-priced lunches, and they often have a large ethnic minority population. Maia's school is 95% African-American.

Maia says that when her students from past classes return to visit, very few of them mention the innovative lessons she taught or the creativity of the instruction. Instead, they mention the love she showed them and the words of motivation she gave them. It reminds her of the Maya Angelou quote, "People will forget what you said; people will forget what you did; but people will never forget how you made them feel."

When Simon asked Maia about how she developed this kind of presence with her students, she said that she became a National Board Certified Teacher in the area of Early Childhood Generalist. This was in addition to her regular state teaching certificate. It allowed her to mentor other teachers in primary education. This kept her knowledgeable about the best practices in primary education and helped her pass it forward to others so that everyone at her school got better at increasing student achievement. She also participated in different learning experiences at the district, state, and national levels.

She credits her principal in supporting her development by allowing her to share at school with staff and other educators in her professional learning community whenever she attended different conferences and workshops. In addition, she was the Social Studies Lead Teacher at her school, which gave her the opportunity to help grow the knowledge of her school colleagues about best instructional practices and to help the school increase student achievement in social studies content (M. Stephen, personal communication, December 18, 2015).

Andy Hargreaves and Michael Fullan (2013) talk about how powerful professional capital is. They advocate that schools think of their teachers as "nation builders" and invest in teacher learning and growth through collaboration. The idea is that team members use each other to develop the capacity and wisdom within the group. Hargreaves and Fullan say that leaders must "push" for more professional capital, "pull" to drive people into their own development with vision and excitement, and "nudge" by offering people choices and guiding them over time to make better and better ones. They say, "Pull wherever you can, push where you must, and nudge all the time" (p. 39). Hargreaves and Fullan believe such an investment yields high returns in prosperity, social cohesion, and social justice—aspirational words, for sure!

Ellie Drago-Severson (2008) believes that teams create a safe place for adults to learn and grow together. Effective teams encourage more open communication. They reduce teacher isolation and increase opportunities for shared leadership. Best of all, they help leaders overcome resistance and enhance implementation of changes.

Recently, Simon was working in Harare, Zimbabwe, and had a chance to meet with one of his mentors, Tudor Bismark. He was introduced to Dr. Oliver Kapepa, an educational consultant, and Jameson Timba, who served as minister of state in the prime minister's office until 2013. Simon asked these men about education in Africa. They felt that teacher training was a way to change teacher mindset. Timba said that in the past, the syllabus was only known by the teacher. It was their power and it was up to the students to figure it out. But Timba offered a new approach: We must change how teachers see themselves and their role. They are more than conveyors of knowledge. They frame the content and create learning *experiences* so that students can meet high expectations. And he saw technology as a way to engage students in new and fresh ways (J. Timba, personal communication, December 12, 2015).

Connie Yowell, CEO of Collective Shift, says, "Learning must be turned into a lifestyle. Too often our current educational system is organized around the consumption of information and making sure kids consume what teachers know and put it back on a test" (Asa, 2015).

So as educational leaders, how do we engage our teachers so that they *want to* participate in ongoing, collaborative learning?

Ellie Drago-Severson (2008) says that in teams, adults make sense of their experiences in developmentally different ways. Some are concrete learners and think in terms of how an issue or experience affects them personally. They need to be pushed to consider the perspectives of others as well. Other adults are more abstract in their thinking but tend to automatically adopt the perspective of another, especially an expert. Their growing edge is to articulate their own perspective before they adopt another's. And then there are the self-authoring learners. They generate their own value system and take responsibility for it. But they need to learn to recognize that other people can legitimately hold opposing perspectives that could inform their own. When leaders understand the kinds of developmental diversity within their teams, they can be intentional about creating safe places for adults to share their perspectives, challenge each other's thinking, and provide a context for growth.

Upgrade the Skill and Infuse the Will Matrix

Max Landsberg includes a business management tool in his book, *The Tao of Coaching* (2009). In business, managers use Landsberg's tool to determine the best management approach for a given staff person. We have adapted it to help educators in formal and informal roles analyze the skill levels and motivational needs of colleagues with whom they work. (See page 58.)

We see it as a tool to help develop and support individuals to work more effectively in teams. In our view, the model shows a way to operationalize Drago-Severson's theory by considering the will of individuals to function within a team compared to their skill level for the work itself. It gives leaders guidance to support the development of individuals without micromanaging the work of the team.

Team members with low motivation and low skill need direction and encouragement to create some quick wins. On the other hand, team members who have low morale but high skill will require a leader to inspire and motivate them, reconnecting them to why they chose to teach in the first place. Team members with low skill but high will (often our best new teachers) need training, feedback, and encouragement to take smart risks to develop their confidence. And the best team members are the ones with high will and high skill. These are the women and men who break sound barriers and lead without title. Leaders draw from this last group to become the shapers of the culture.

	Low Skill	High Skill
High Will	**GUIDE** • Offer low-risk opportunities to grow and learn. • Provide tools, training, coaching, and feedback about what they are doing well. • Relax judgment and control as you recognize progress.	**DELEGATE** • Recognize them and communicate your trust in them. • Help them develop stretch goals, broaden their responsibilities, and treat them as "partners." • Give broad latitude for them to experiment, allowing them to share their experiences and mentor others. • Help them become the shapers of the culture.
Low Will	**DIRECT** • Get to know individuals personally and assume positive intent. • Help them create a vision for their work. • Structure quick wins, train/coach patiently, supervise with frequent feedback about the progress you see, and set clear expectations.	**EXCITE** • Get to know individuals personally, what motivates them, and the values to which they aspire. • Seek to understand "why" they have low will. • Help them reconnect to what drew them into education in the first place. • Look for and provide recognition to reinforce their positive behaviors.

Adapted from Landsberg, M. (2009). *The Tao of Coaching*. London: Profile Books.

Breaking Ranks: The Power of Team Thrust

In a February 2016 interview with Marceta, Jennifer Abrams suggested that a team mindset is quite different from a teacher-as-expert mindset. When forming new teams, individuals may worry about how their expertise compares to the others on the team, and they may wonder if the other team members will respect them. Therefore, it is important for the team to understand the leader's assumptions about why working in teams is important and what their beliefs are for teaming.

A teaming mindset is based on beliefs like these:

- Working with a colleague helps me grow.
- Everyone in the group has something to offer.

- Individuals within the group are all competent and respected members of the school.
- I am continuously forming and growing as an educator.
- The end product will be better by working within a team than if I did it by myself.

In a conversation with leadership coaches facilitated by Karla Reiss (personal communication, February 17, 2016), host of the Educator Community of Practice, sponsored by the International Coach Federation, similar ideas emerged. They emphasized the importance of making ground rules explicit. That is, make agreements clear among team members about how to handle things like how decisions are made and what our purpose is. Encourage members to listen respectfully to each other and take responsibility for contributing to the group from their area of strength.

The coach group suggested that spending time in building trust among the team members was very important, especially at the beginning of team formation. They can do this by sharing leadership tasks among the members and identifying and openly celebrating the strengths of the team. This makes the value of the team visible and encourages members to openly share their gifts and talents. Bob Carter, a coach from Texas, emphasized the importance of team members acknowledging issues and relational problems that arise. "Elephants in the room can consume all the oxygen," he said. "If you don't take them out and play with them, you will have dysfunction" (B. Carter, personal communication, February 17, 2016). To do this, the group needs clear norms about how to disagree without being disagreeable in order to feel safe enough to speak up.

Marceta suggests that teams can even use the "elephants in the room" as windows into understanding what others care about. Robert Kegan, in an interview with Dennis Sparks (2002), asserts that "underneath the surface torrent of complaints, cynical humor, and eye-rolling, there is a hidden river of passion and commitment" (p. 66). By listening deeply to the words the complainer says, team leaders can flip the complaint to understand what that person cares about or needs. This care or need is often something that the whole team desires as well. So then the team leader can respond from a position of understanding and caring rather than adversary because suddenly you are on the same side of the table.

Sharon Newton-Carroll (2016), a vice principal from Ravenswood Middle School in Ravenswood, West Virginia, illustrates this well. Their school received Breakthrough School recognition in 2010. She tells about how her school math team began to understand the resistance of parents "in the holler" to homework for the students. At first her math team members were angry about the fact that parents would tell their children not to worry about the math homework—it wasn't important. The students told their math teachers, "It don't matter. Dad told us doing our chores with the animals is more important." The teachers were appalled and angry. How could they help lift these kids out of poverty if they didn't have the support of the parents? What was wrong with these parents?

But as the math team analyzed more deeply what was underneath the parent attitude, they came to realize that homework exposed the parents to revealing how little they themselves knew about new math concepts. The parents were not prepared to help the students with math and did not want to show their vulnerability and limitations to their children. What an insight! Now the team could strategize about how to provide homework support within an expanded school day or in extracurricular time and run parent workshops to suggest ways to support their child's learning without having to assist with specific assignments. Parents could ask about school work, show an interest in how their child was doing in classes, show up at school academic events (as they do for athletic events), and provide a place and time for the child to read and study at home without having to be responsible to oversee the work.

This made all the difference. No longer were teachers blaming the parents. They understood the need: Provide the tutoring assistance onsite before and after school, and sponsor parent information events that would help parents show interest without needing to have answers. They could all be on the same side of the table supporting student learning.

Here's another Breaking Ranks® example. Principal Robbie Hooker, 2013 Breakthrough School recipient, transformed his school faculty at Clarke Central High School in Clarke County, Georgia, from door-closed, teaching-in-isolation to collaborative teams. Robbie says it all started when Phillip Lanoue arrived as the new superintendent. He met with all faculty and declared, "We will no longer use poverty as an excuse for why our students can't succeed." He invited the staff to shift away from seeing students through the lens of poverty and instead see them as fully capable of achieving awesome results! This was the aspirational message that Robbie needed to get his faculty onboard to help all students be successful. He started with leading a whole-faculty study group of *Breaking Ranks II: Strategies for Leading High School Reform*. What the faculty learned in that experience caused them to want to immediately change the school master schedule to better meet the needs of all the students. With that change, Robbie was able to form collaborative planning teams for teachers of like subjects. This allowed teachers to develop lesson plans and to review data to ensure students were learning. The school also moved away from resource classes for special needs students and offered more inclusive classes. And Robbie challenged his veteran Advanced Placement teachers to teach some of the most at-risk students because they had various tools in their teaching toolboxes to help *all* the students be successful.

Robbie points to the importance of networking with other successful school leaders across the country through associations like the NASSP and their state affiliate in Georgia. At these experiences, he was able to see other leaders working in high-poverty schools and getting positive results. They did not use poverty as an excuse. Having candid conversations with other high school principals in high-poverty locations helped him realize that his students in poverty were able to be successful in Honors and Advanced Placement classes if teachers provided support and were able to scaffold the curriculum. Robbie's school has seen a dramatic increase in the number of minority students who have taken the challenge of enrolling in Honors and Advanced Placement courses. This school has also started a Gifted Minority Achievement Focus Group. The mission of this group is to empower, educate, and support the *parents* of culturally diverse students about the various opportunities at the school for their high-achieving students. The overall goal is to ensure that students from culturally diverse backgrounds have equal access to all opportunities that provide success in secondary and postsecondary education.

Robbie's advice for other principals who want to replicate this kind of model is to first gain the trust of the faculty and staff and focus on the instructional practices taking place in classrooms. Robbie says the primary mission of principals is providing teachers with the support they need to be successful in the classroom—even when 74% of the students are living in poverty (R. Hooker, personal communication, February 25, 2016).

Where's the Fuel? It's All About the SCARF Experience

Teamwork is very important because it shapes the culture of the school. When people work effectively in teams, the individuals on the team build strong emotional connections with each other. These connections transcend analytics, agendas, and resisters who don't want to change. Teams become the glue supporting transformative cultures. For these reasons, it is vital to help individuals learn the interpersonal and communication skills that will support them to function well in a team setting. Yet very little of our degree preparation and certification coursework focuses on helping educators learn what adults need to work well together.

This is where David Rock's (2008) work is so valuable. Rock is a neuroscientist by trade who filtered through countless studies to try to determine how to influence others and build engagement. He determined that it all boils down to a simple acronym: SCARF—Status, Certainty, Autonomy, Relatedness, and Fairness. According to Rock, the brain plays a key role in determining whether individuals view someone as friend or foe. In essence, one's brain uses the SCARF variables as an organizing principle. Those things that increase Status, Certainty, Autonomy, Relatedness, and Fairness put a person into what Rock calls a "Maximum Reward State of Mind." This state of mind is synonymous with engagement.

On the flip side, all things that decrease the SCARF variables produce a "Danger" response, which drives down engagement.

David Rock's model gives leaders guidance about how to set the tone, influence the level of engagement, and support relationship building within teams. Principals can model and coach team leaders about how to use the SCARF elements in facilitating their teams.

Marceta also writes about other important communication skills that support good functioning within teams. The foundation of this communication is committed listening. It is doing more than just hearing the words. It is also listening deeply to understand the emotion and the meaning underneath. It shows you care about other people, you respect them, and you are trying to understand their message.

SCARF: The Interpersonal and Communication Skills That Support Team Functioning

Status comes into play as individuals compare themselves to those around them. If the leader comes in as "expert," individuals on the team may feel diminished or threatened. They may argue or resist new ideas as a way to show their own knowledge or expertise.

Instead, first notice what individuals are doing well. Ask their opinions and perspectives on ideas and tasks. Build on the contributions they offer. In this way, the leader shows individuals they are respected and valued members of the team, and individuals will feel like equal partners within the team.

Certainty comes by setting clear expectations for the purpose and tasks of the team. It explains "why" and "what," creating boundaries and understanding for the work. If the "why" and "what" are not clear for the leader, then share what *is* known and when others might expect more information. It's all about making expectations and goals explicit.

Autonomy comes by giving individuals choice and control over their work. Build in choices wherever you can. This helps individuals feel they have some control over aspects of the work. Use choice as a way to raise and lower stress among the members. For example, a leader could say, "You have to do this, but you get to choose *when to* do it over the next two weeks."

Relatedness begins to develop the minute individuals meet someone new. Our brains are programmed to determine very quickly if you are a friend or foe. Create ways to help individuals bond and feel comfortable within the group, especially when the team is first forming. Open meetings with handshakes and some personal sharing. Help the group develop ground rules about "the way we want to work together." And when beginning new tasks or assignments, smiles, sharing, and warm-up activities are valuable to reinforce feelings of safety. All of these small actions increase positive feelings of *we* as a team.

Finally, **Fairness** is about how team members treat each other. Leaders who are perceived as fair model how to treat others, are transparent in their motives, and are open in their communication with team members. Give more information than necessary, if you can. Be open in your communication and clear about who and what influences your decisions. If you don't take a team recommendation, help them understand the reasons for the decision you made. Individuals may not agree with you, but they will begin to trust your honesty (Rock, 2008).

In addition, it is very helpful if team members learn to always assume positive intention on the part of their colleagues. Assuming positive intent means that team members are careful about their interpretations of the behaviors and actions of others. The Wilson brothers (Wilson & Wilson, 2004), in their book *Play to Win,* say, "Whenever something happens and you begin to say, 'This means…,' you are making stuff up" (p. 107). Instead of having only one interpretation of a bad action, seek a diversity of other interpretations. Assume benevolence (or forgetfulness, or having a bad day) rather than intentional harm. This helps you keep your emotions in check and show up as the person you want to be.

When leaders empower others, they provide clear expectations, let the team make many decisions, and are careful to treat everyone fairly. In this way, they help build trust and rapport within the team. When teams function well, staff members become smarter, more engaged, and more productive in their work. They also become more connected and invested in your leadership. But when teams work poorly, staff members become alienated, disengaged, and less productive.

FROM OUR FLIGHT JOURNAL: JACIE MASLYK, FORMER PRINCIPAL, PITTSBURGH, PA

Positive Peer Pressure

Jacie Maslyk, former principal at Hopewell Area School District in Pittsburgh, PA, speaks about positive peer pressure. This is when there is so much emphasis about who is doing innovative instruction that it positively impacts student learning. All the teachers begin to feel the urge to join in as more and more colleagues begin to try out improved instructional practices, technology enhancements, and innovative classroom environments.

Jacie encouraged the innovators to share the strategies with others, colleague to colleague. She also rewarded risk takers with a positive note, additional materials or resources, extra time to further a project, or other ways that were the most meaningful to them. As a result, more and more teachers began trying new things. Positive peer pressure for innovation became almost contagious in her building. Teachers were grabbing up new ideas and putting themselves out there to try them. Almost everyone was moving forward to make classrooms, the school, or district better. Those who didn't, decided to go elsewhere. The positive peer pressure in her building created an environment that made the brilliance of positive teachers the norm not the exception (J. Maslyk, personal communication, July 7, 2016).

We humans are complex creatures. We want to be known, seen, and respected by others. Brilliant leaders strive to do more than communicate a message. They are intentional about always *connecting* with people.

They do this in two ways:

- Being genuinely curious about staff members. Ask more questions about staff members' likes and their lives. Show an interest in individuals on a personal level.
- Being humble. People love authenticity, so be frank, transparent, and caring. Share personal things about yourself while you are learning about others. Leaders who rule with an iron hand tend to portray themselves as better than the rest. Not only does that make the leader seem obnoxious, it leads to resentment from the staff. People work better for those who let others see them as a person rather than a title.

Call to Action: Execute Your Flight Plan

Select among the exercises to help you assess and develop your team. The first one will help you and your team members assess the assets of your team and consider how to use them to your best advantage.

Exercise 3.1: Is Your Team an Asset or Liability?

The public today expects high performance from schools, educators, and students. For this reason, our teams need staff at all levels who are assets (people who contribute value) rather than liabilities (people who are disengaged or drawbacks) in planning robust instruction for students.

Are you getting the maximum value from your staff members? Are you tapping into their desire to be high-value assets by using their minds to create greater student engagement and learning?

How can you help them bring more *professional presence* to their teamwork? Help them see the value in being thinking-intensive workers: men and women who use their intangible assets—their knowledge, skills, relationships, and talent—to drive student learning.

Step 1 Think about yourself and your team. List their names or initials below.	**Step 2** List the unique intangible asset (knowledge, skill, talent, etc.) each person can offer the team. Be concise and specific.	**Step 3** As a leader, identify how you can leverage their assets to generate the greatest impact for engaging students with instruction.
NF	Knows how to use Guided Reading process very effectively.	Ask her to present Guided Reading at a faculty meeting to help move this instructional strategy into more classrooms.
RM	Is excellent in building relationships with challenging young boys.	Ask him to share one of his stories of connecting to a tough kid and explain why he thinks it worked with the student. Then ask him to apply this insight to setting higher learning expectations for young boys.

Exercise 3.2: Skill Versus Will Analysis

The Skill Versus Will matrix helps answer two simple, yet important questions:

- How much can the person rely on his or her skills to complete the task?
- How much does that person really want to complete the task?

Analyze your staff using our Skill Versus Will model. How can this data help you tailor your conversations with individual faculty members? Who are the people in the high skill/high will quadrant whom you could tap for more leadership responsibility?

Think about two or three teachers you are currently working with. Analyze where they might be on the model. How could this model help you to work with these individuals?

High Will	**GUIDE** • Offer low-risk opportunities to grow and learn. • Provide tools, training, coaching, and feedback about what they are doing well. • Relax judgment and control as you recognize progress.	**DELEGATE** • Recognize them and communicate your trust in them. • Help them develop stretch goals, broaden their responsibilities, and treat them as "partners." • Give broad latitude for them to experiment, allowing them to share their experiences and mentor others. • Help them become the shapers of the culture.
Low Will	**DIRECT** • Get to know individuals personally and assume positive intent. • Help them create a vision for their work. • Structure quick wins, train/coach patiently, supervise with frequent feedback about the progress you see, and set clear expectations.	**EXCITE** • Get to know individuals personally, what motivates them, and the values to which they aspire. • Seek to understand "why" they have low will. • Help them reconnect to what drew them into education in the first place. • Look for and provide recognition to reinforce their positive behaviors.
	Low Skill	**High Skill**

Adapted from Landsberg, M. (2009). *The Tao of Coaching*. London: Profile Books.

Exercise 3.3: Reframing Complaints

When you are faced with a recurring complaint from your staff, parents, or community, use this exercise to figure out what people are really asking for underneath the surface words. It will help you address what they care about when you respond, instead of getting into a debate about the complaint on the surface.

Think about a person (colleague, school parent, friend, or family member) who is always complaining to you about an issue.

Column 1	Column 2	Column 3	Column 4	Column 5
Exact words	**Underlying worry/fear**	**Care about?**	**Where is the win-win (sweet spot)?**	**How to start?**
What are some of the exact words the person uses in the complaint?	Think deeply about what could be the underlying fear, worry, or emotion that is really behind the concern.	Flip the fear, worry, or emotion to create a positive statement about what the person cares about.	What does this tell you about a strength or positive characteristic the person has that you could also agree with?	What is a way to start a conversation, seeing the complainer as having a legitimate perspective, and speaking about what he *really* cares about?
Student failed a test: "worked hard, teacher isn't any good, child very discouraged, wants to drop the class or change teachers"	*Parent wants child to do well in school. Fear that teacher doesn't like his child so not being fair.*	*Parent cares that his child and teacher have a strong, positive relationship. (Wants teacher to love his child as much as he does)*	*He understands the importance of having a strong, positive relationship with teachers.* *Sweet spot is focusing on building that relationship.*	*"I hear the frustration in your voice and I'm wondering if you are really worrying that the teacher doesn't like your child."*

Visit www.releasingleadershipbrilliance.com to watch the Chapter 3 author video: "How You Can Harness the Power of Team Thrust."

Student Brilliance—Soars When You "Reduce Drag"

Build the Student Versus the Profile

Leadership Brilliance is about more than activating the brilliance of the adults in a school. It is also about reducing the barriers that keep students from tapping into their brilliance. We call this *Reducing Drag*. *Drag* is the aerodynamic force that opposes an aircraft's motion through the air. *Drag* creates resistance that slows down an aircraft. In schools, drag represents all the barriers (intentional and unintentional) that hold back students from engaging fully in their work, learning at their peak, and blossoming into full potential.

Recently Simon spoke to students at Orange Lutheran High School in Orange County, California. The parents of these students are titans of business—Hollywood moguls and the top 1% of income earners in the United States. Parents expect their children to get into the top universities in the country and complain loudly to teachers when their children receive bad grades. The principal, Leslie Smith, and her faculty described the students as being stressed, anxious, and under intense pressure.

The faculty leadership team at Orange Lutheran worry that their students are too focused on getting into college and therefore not living in the present. So many are more concerned with grades than with learning, and they are trying to excel in as many different extra-curricular activities as possible rather than enjoying the activities themselves. Rather than enjoying their high school experience, they are set on building their resumes and enhancing their profiles for college applications. It was all about resumes and profiles, not about *learning* (L. Smith, personal communication, March 24, 2016).

Whether students attend schools in struggling inner-city communities or wealthy private enclaves, drag can be a problem.

Warning Signs of Student Disengagement

What are the signs of *Drag* in our schools? We see it in the students' faces and the feelings they express when we ask them what their experience of school is: boredom, stress, fear of failure, feeling schoolwork is a grind, and lacking resilience, with hopelessness that the future can be better. We see this in the results of the Gallup Student Poll, given to U.S. students in Grades 5 through12. Shane Lopez, chief architect of the Poll, says, "Hope, engagement, and well-being are significantly related to student performance, influencing outcomes such as grades, credits earned, achievement scores, likelihood to stay in school, and future employment" (Lopez, 2014). Although the results of the poll aren't representative of the U.S. student population, they do illuminate how more than half a million young people feel about the quality of their lives, their experiences at school, and their future.

In the fall of 2013, more than 600,000 students completed the poll. Although 54% of students surveyed were hopeful, 32% felt stuck in their lives, and 14% were discouraged about the future. In looking at engagement, 55% reported being engaged with school, but 28% reported not being engaged and 17% reported being actively *disengaged*. Only 33% of the students taking the poll reported having all three characteristics of being truly success ready; that is, they reported being hopeful, engaged, and thriving (Lopez, 2014).

Lopez (2014) also noted that looking at the polling results as students progress through school, juniors in high school rated their current lives as worse than seventh graders did. Students become less engaged as each school year passes, making schools home to what Lopez calls "psychological dropouts." High school students report that their days seem less interesting and more exhausting than younger students do. Over time, students' feelings of being treated with respect, interest in things at school, and energy decrease.

In Chapter 1 you read the story of Simon's children who, despite having all the advantages of a private school and supportive parents, often seemed to be just going through the motions of school without real energy or excitement. Marceta, too, has a granddaughter who is one of the psychological dropouts that Lopez (2014) identified. The granddaughter just turned 16, is a high school sophomore, and has no interest in school. It's a struggle to get her to attend each day and complete minimal tasks to keep from flunking. She would be among those in the Gallup poll reporting themselves as being "actively disengaged." Lopez's work shows us that even though many students are doing well in our schools, there are still almost half of them who are just floating along, doing OK, but not thriving—and certainly not working in ways that tap into their full potential. Meeting the motivational needs of only half of our children is not good enough. This chapter will offer some ideas and guidance on steps you can take to further engage and motivate all of your students.

Drag Data You Should Know

What do we know about factors that increase student engagement and reduce drag?

Carol Dweck (2006) talks about the importance of students having a growth mindset: a belief that the harder you work at something, the better you will be at it. That is different than a fixed mindset, which assumes intelligence and basic abilities are fixed traits. Students' mindsets predict their motivation as well as their achievement level in the learning process.

Gravity Goldberg (2016) tells teachers that the traditional classroom roles of assigner, monitor, and manager limit the student's role to being compliant. She says that if teachers want to empower their students to actively engage in their own learning, they need to shift to four new roles:

- Miner: uncovering what and how students work (informal assessment).
- Mirror: telling students what they already know how to do (giving feedback).
- Model: showing students what to do to help their learning (demonstration).
- Mentor: helping students find new ways to learn that work for them (guided practice and coaching).

By embracing these four new roles, teachers can transform their classrooms from teacher-directed to student-centered. Their classrooms will become places where students make choices, reflect on those choices, and become decision makers about what works best for their learning.

Researchers also talk about grit and resilience as being important factors in the engagement of students in their own learning. Angela Duckworth (2013) loosely defines grit as persistence over time to overcome challenges and accomplish big goals. It is a good predictor of GPA and graduation rates. Twenty-five years of research has shown that giving students challenging goals encourages greater effort and persistence than providing moderate, "do-your-best" goals or no goals at all. But simply setting a high bar is not enough. Students also need the *will* to achieve goals, a *belief* that they can become smarter and turn failure into success through their own efforts, and the ability to *delay gratification* so they can stay focused on the task at hand (Goodwin & Miller, 2013).

Resilience is another concept that is important to reducing drag. Resilience is a set of attributes such as feelings of competence, belonging, usefulness, and personal control. Resilience provides students with the strength and fortitude to not give up when the work gets difficult or when they fail at first. Instead, they reengage, look for help, and try again. They have a hopeful and optimistic attitude that they will eventually get the job done.

In schools we can structure opportunities into daily routines that enable students to experience these feelings of resiliency and grit:

- Provide them with authentic evidence of academic success (competence);
- Show them they are valued members of the class (belonging);
- Recognize times when they make real contributions to the class (usefulness);
- Make them feel empowered by giving them choices about their learning (personal control) (Sagor, 1996).

Russ Quaglia and Michael Corso (2014) did extensive work in the area of student voice. They interviewed 66,000 students in Grades 6 through 12 and found that 47% felt they had voice and 43% thought that school was boring. Quaglia and Corso connected student voice to the development of student self-worth, engagement, and purpose. When students have a voice, they know they matter. This invites them to become active partners in their own education. They see a purpose for their education and begin to understand how their education will lead to what they want to become. Quaglia speaks passionately about giving students voice in our schools. He says that when students know the goals of the class, believe they have a voice, and believe that the teacher is willing to learn from them, they are seven times more likely to be motivated to learn whatever the teacher is teaching. Engagement is about getting the whole child—head, heart, and hands—engaged in the learning. It is about fostering the use of imagination when students are interacting with information. That's not about *entertaining* students but about providing the tools and resources for them to be the attention center of their own learning.

Finally, in order to promote engagement, Quaglia and Corso (2014) urge educators to encourage healthy risk-taking—challenging students to set big goals and persist in the learning until they feel successful. When students think they can be successful and believe the *teacher* thinks they can be successful, they are eight times more likely to be motivated to learn than students who don't have those beliefs.

FROM OUR FLIGHT JOURNAL: BRAD GUSTAFSON, ELEMENTARY PRINCIPAL, PLYMOUTH, MN

And a Child Shall Lead Us

Brad Gustafson, principal at Greenwood Elementary School, Plymouth, Minnesota, tells a story about a 6-year-old in one of his kindergarten classrooms. The children in the class were playing with a robot that wasn't working properly. The teacher asked the children, "How can we fix it?" A 6-year-old answered, "Why don't we ask Twitter?" The classmates asked Twitter and that started a dialogue with the company, which eventually shipped the class a BeBot to build. The 6-year-old and his classmates put it together themselves. Acting as agents of their own learning, making a plan and executing it, interacting with the real world, and receiving a response truly empowered the learners! After this experience they were more likely to soar—to take initiative in their own learning and speak out about their ideas (B. Gustafson, personal communication, July 7, 2016).

John Hattie (2012), in his book *Visible Learning for Teachers*, did an extensive meta-analysis of the effects of the major contributors to learning—student characteristics, home effects, school effects, teacher characteristics, curricular programs, and teaching strategies. He looked at more than 60,000 research studies involving more than 88 million people. Hattie found that one of the stronger predictors of student achievement was the teachers' relationships with each other. When teachers worked collaboratively in teams to understand their impact on learning, the effect size on student achievement was .93 (compared to .4 effect size to attain the typical one year of academic growth). As teachers worked together to evaluate their impact on student learning, they were diagnosing and planning instruction that was just right for the learning of each student. And they were designing ways to help students see errors as opportunities for growth in learning. This focused, collaborative work in professional teams could result in more than two years of academic growth for students in just one school year! These findings also correlate to the attributes of "professional capital" that Hargreaves and Fullan (2013) identified and the "social capital" that Leana (2011) found to be so important to increasing student achievement in our schools.

Another important attribute to increasing student achievement that Hattie (2012) found was the teacher's relationship with the student. The effect size of this attribute on student achievement was .72. Once again, Hattie was showing that a strong, positive teacher relationship with students can result in almost two years of academic growth in one school year!

However, Brad Gustafson, principal at Greenwood Elementary School in Plymouth, MN, cautions educators to not let building relationships be an end in itself. He says,

> *It's the* foundation *of learning, yet it's what you* do *with that foundation that truly matters. Relationship building is only the beginning for learning. It can never be graded nor will it show up as a bubble on an assessment. But it can connect adults to students in ways that help them dream bigger and go where they want to go.* (B. Gustafson, personal communication, July 7, 2016)

Connect the Dots: Real School Examples

Here are some examples of how leaders successfully turned around failing schools by focusing on reducing drag and breaking sound barriers for students.

When Matt Saferite became principal of Ramay Junior High in Fayetteville, Arkansas, slightly more than 60% of his students were passing the state assessments. Something needed to change, and he was committed to different outcomes for the students in his school.

He started the turnaround of his school with three deeply held personal beliefs:

- Every student wants to do his or her best all the time.
- He can't motivate students; he can only find out what demotivates them and stop doing it (thereby stopping drag!).
- His role as principal was to model with staff what he wanted his teachers to do with students.

Matt used the works of W. Edwards Deming and Will Glasser around student voice, John Hattie's (2012) work about visible learning, and the Gallup Strengths Finder research to become the foundational pieces of his school's turnaround. He became avid about getting to know students even before they entered his school. He surveyed incoming eighth graders and studied their student demographics and needs as a way of seeing what students perceive as a drag on their learning. He continues to be adamant that all student programs must be reviewed several times each year to incorporate new student interests and needs.

During the school year, he collects a random sample of student satisfaction surveys *every other* week. Using Survey Monkey, approximately 25 students (about 6 students from each grade and of each gender) are randomly identified to take the survey each time. The data are collected and grouped, and the staff and leadership teams have conversations about it. They look for trends and gaps, as well as "flipping the complaints" to learn what the students care about. Matt and his teachers use the data to proactively improve students' satisfaction with their schooling and to ascertain trends and solve problem or issues that seem to be arising.

He has counselors collect not only academic and personal data for the students but also career data for them. Even at the middle level, it is really important for these young students to dream and aspire to what comes after high school. Teachers and staff help feed aspirations about getting into college or going for a good-paying trade or technical job. Middle school is not too early to be having these kinds of conversations. Matt's experience as an administrator at an eleventh- and twelfth-grade senior high campus reinforced the importance of these kinds of early conversations with young people about life after high school graduation.

At the same time Matt was growing student voice in the school, he was sharing John Hattie's (2012) work about visible learning with teachers. Hattie found that one of the stronger predictors of student achievement was the teachers' relationship with the students. So Matt challenged his teachers to imagine what it would look like if *every* student succeeded. And he asked them to focus on building a student-centered culture within the school *before* they worried about test scores.

The results were amazing. The student proficiency rate on the state literacy exam increased to more than 80% and more than 90% on the end-of-course Algebra I exam (which all students completed in either their eighth- or ninth-grade year). All students (100%) scored "proficient" or "advanced" on the end-of-course geometry exam, and the staff worked to more than double the number of students completing geometry by the end of ninth grade.

In addition, the staff at Ramay Junior High implemented a ninth-grade biology course at a time when biology was typically a tenth-grade course in Arkansas. Since the first year, 100% of the students pass the end-of-course biology exam with "proficient" or "advanced" scores, and the number of students enrolling in the course has consistently and significantly increased.

As these standardized test scores increased, the performance of the subpopulations (Hispanic, African-American, special education, 504, free or reduced-price meal eligible students, etc.) measured by the Arkansas Department of Education all increased to the point of a near elimination of any performance gap. Due to the efforts of staff and students that resulted in these standardized testing results, the school was named a NASSP Breakthrough School in 2011 (M. Saferite, personal communication, February 25, 2016).

For Matt, this transformation began when he became crystal clear about his belief that every student really *wanted* to do his or her best. Then he set about challenging teachers to take the actions that would enable *every* student to succeed. He focused on building a *culture* of using staff and student strengths, a culture of allowing all people in the building to do their best work every day. That emphasis on maximizing strengths included a significant focus on student voice. By regularly listening to students about their experience of school, staff were able to use students' perspectives about drag to make important changes.

Matt focused on building relationships with students and modeled for teachers how they could interact with students to develop strong, positive relationships. Students *and* teachers became more engaged in building *partner* relationships with each other around the learning process.

Another good example is Sheena Alaiasa, now principal at Kamehameha Schools in Honolulu, HI. Prior to this new opportunity, she was principal at King Intermediate School in Kane'ohe, HI, where she led the school out of restructuring—the harshest sanction under the No Child Left Behind law—elevating it to statewide recognition as a Strive HI Award recipient and one of only seven schools in Hawaii to close the achievement gap. In 2014, Sheena was named NASSP Middle School Principal of the Year.

Her amazing achievements have been realized despite her humble beginnings. She was born and raised beside a prison camp in New Zealand and came to the United States chasing a career in the tourism industry. Along the way she learned she was good at teaching, so she switched careers. Eventually she became a principal at King Intermediate School, a very low-performing school in a community known for drug usage and trafficking. In one of the faculty meetings, she heard that "these kids don't want to learn; learning is not their priority." It was all about getting money to support their families through cock fighting or selling drugs, and that's when she decided she had to teach her students that they have choices: to stay in the environment they are in now, or choose to build something else.

She had to shift the focus of the faculty to concentrate on the Five Rs (Relationships, Respect, Resourcefulness, Resiliency, and Responsibility), which helped students and teachers create a school based on values and the belief that these students had worth and were important. Students began to grow into this belief, and they found themselves excelling in school and had the confidence to graduate from high school and go to college.

Sheena created an acronym that clearly communicated her expectations: SAM. It stood for Student Achievement Matters. She inspired staff to reach down and pull up students. They needed to be the ones to show students they were worth caring about!

Sheena exhorted teachers to give students experiences in learning—not just talk to them. She wanted them to show children the excitement of learning and what it feels like to grow in their learning. Staff started to respond by focusing on engaging students in their learning. It worked. In just four years, the school turned around and moved from restructuring to statewide recognition!

Now Sheena is at Kamehameha Schools and continues to inspire teachers to help students *experience* learning. At the new school, there was a physics teacher who had come from the business world. He was very knowledgeable but used lectures and tests as his primary approach to teaching. This was a drag on the students' learning because they didn't have enough experience to make useful meaning of it. The teacher kept saying, "I just don't know what you mean by giving students experiences in learning. I think that is what I am doing!"

So Sheena decided she had to find a model for him to see what experiences in learning looked like. In other words, she had to make this teacher's learning an experience for him! There was another physics teacher in the building who was masterful at making the content meaningful and fun for the students. She and the traditional teacher observed the other teacher teach a lesson on the physics of the pendulum.

When they entered the room they saw the students gathered in teams. A large, weighted ball was suspended from the ceiling and swinging from side to side, while the teacher was singing to cranked up pop music. The students were measuring the distances and path of each pendulum swing and loving it! They were fully engaged in the learning as well as seeing application and context at the same time.

Afterward, Sheena and the traditional physics teacher debriefed about the experience. "Now I get it!" he said. It was about connecting the content to the students in meaningful, even fun ways. "Engagement" wasn't about showmanship and entertainment; it was about communicating your own passion and energy for the content—answering the student's question, Why should I care? From then on, the traditional physics teacher began planning instruction differently so that he, too, could engage the students with the content he loved (S. Alaiasa, personal communication, December 2, 2015).

Here's our final example of how a school looks when the staff focuses on reducing the drag within achievement gaps. Mater Academy Charter School is a 2011 NASSP Breakthrough School in Hialeah Gardens, FL. Judy Marty is the principal of the school, which serves students in Grades 6 through 12. Eighty percent of the families at her school cannot speak English and 83% live in poverty. Society does not expect her students to succeed.

When Judy was first hired as principal of the charter school, she had to get her staff past the thinking that "these kids cannot learn." It was causing a terrible drag on the students' learning. Her teachers told her that these kids could not do this "rigor stuff." So she took them to places where it was working. She told them, "You have to go deeper. You cannot just *cover* the material. What are the standards? Go deeper! You can't just use the same lesson plans as before!" (J. Marty, personal communication, February 25, 2016).

She envisioned the academy as a school that assumed every child was going to college or postsecondary school. As people enter the school, the first thing they see is a College Wall. It shows a picture of *every senior* and where he or she was accepted for college or postsecondary schooling. As the year progresses, they begin to include the scholarship offers coming to current seniors. Judy also has an Alumni Wall showing "Where in the World Are Mater Alums?" This inspires all Mater students to dream big.

As students begin the academy, staff model grit and resilience by telling students they will have more homework and stay at school longer each day than kids at other schools. The school doors open at 6 AM each day and close after 7 PM. There are activities before and after school and tutoring for every class that is offered. They also have Saturday tutoring classes and summer library hours.

For adults, they have monthly book studies for parents as well as staff. The expectation is that everybody is continuously learning. And the results are dramatic: 97% of the students graduate on time and 92% go on to college or postsecondary school.

Mater Academy is a large school with a small-school atmosphere. They seek to build strong associations with the students and their families. Relationships with counselors, faculty, staff, coaches, and club sponsors are personalized and often extend well beyond the regular school day. In all aspects of life at Mater, the teachers use a push-pull philosophy to develop grit and resilience in the students:

- They push students to challenge themselves to go above their perceived limits;
- They pull students to achieve beyond their expectations.

Judy and her assistant principals each challenge themselves to do 15 walk-throughs a day! She believes you must inspect what you expect. Sure enough, after this practice started, instruction dramatically improved.

Judy strongly believes in professional learning, encouraging staff to attend conferences and workshops and share their new insights when they return. This builds confidence and offers opportunity for peer-to-peer learning. When teachers have a challenging student, she encourages them to network with other teachers to find creative classroom management solutions, once again modeling resilience for the staff.

Teachers constantly look at student data to guide their instruction. The department chairs have common planning time and coordinate common instructional issues across content areas. Everything they teach, they tutor.

In 2014, the school was investigated for test fraud by state and federal government officials because their test results were "illogical." Ninety-seven percent of their students passed the Florida state exam and 179 of the approximately 500 Mater students who took the test passed with a "5" rating, which is the highest score. Investigators said the students were too poor to have these kinds of scores. Angered and annoyed, Judy and her staff endured intense scrutiny of the school's testing preparation, environment, and staff. After many months of investigation, the school was finally exonerated. What infuriated Judy most was the attitude that poor kids cannot achieve to these high levels.

How do Judy and her staff get these kinds of results? They set high expectations for every student who enrolls. Many seventh graders are taking ninth-grade credit courses. They offer 23 Advanced Placement (AP) courses and mandatory SAT test prep for all eleventh graders. At graduation, many students have already simultaneously earned their associate degree because of dual credit coursework offered. Judy is proud that Mater staff works hard to reduce drag on rigorous student learning by helping *everyone* dream big and dig deep into challenging work with grit and resilience.

Judy and her staff want the students to aspire to high levels of learning. Ninety-five percent of eighth graders who take the High School Florida Algebra I end-of-course exam achieve passing scores. Similarly, for the High School Biology exam, the majority of eighth graders who take the test pass. Even when students do not earn passing scores, students are expected to stretch their learning goals, and the experience gives them a glimpse of what more they will need to know in order to pass the next year. They are taught that "not passing" is not a failure. It is another opportunity for students to learn resilience by figuring out what they need to know in order to get to where they want to go.

It is the same with offering AP courses. When the school first started offering AP courses, only 5% of the students were passing at the AP criteria level. Now 50% pass at that level. Students are taught not only the AP content but also the grit, persistence, and engagement they need to pass at the AP level. The faculty is now experimenting with offering Honors Algebra I and Honors Geometry at the same time for eighth graders, with excellent results.

The school engages the whole family in the learning experiences of their children by offering special programs for students and parents to support the academic progress of the children:

- Hosting sessions to explain graduation requirements for sixth-grade students and parents,
- Having "Do the Right Thing" sessions to support development of moral judgment,
- Hosting sessions for subject selection guidance and help,
- Providing onsite individual and group counseling sessions,
- Sponsoring "Data Talk" sessions with parents,
- Hosting College Fairs at the school for juniors and seniors,
- Pulling seniors as needed into "No Senior Left Behind" sessions,
- Hosting sessions about dual enrollment courses, and
- Hosting AP Course Fairs for eighth graders for recruiting and orientation.

The culture of the school is that *every* student is important. The leadership team, including all assistant principals and team leaders of professional learning communities, meets every two weeks to talk about what students need to make this goal happen. At the beginning, the teachers complained about all the meetings. But it ended up empowering them because they began to look for and brainstorm ideas to bring to the table. And Judy says, "If you bring an idea, you are in charge of it!" (J. Marty, personal communication, February 25, 2016). This is how Judy reduces drag at her school. Every teacher takes personal responsibility for the success of his or her group of students. Judy listens, then empowers her staff to move forward on the ideas that energize them and meet the needs of the students. Students get "surround sound" support for their learning.

Connecting the Dots to the World of Work

Yong Zhao, author of *World Class Learners: Educating Creative and Entrepreneurial Students* (2012), exhorts schools to reduce drag by creating an environment that supports individual growth and opportunities for individuals to develop their talents, passions, and interests. In our research we found some interesting public/private partnerships that did just that. NAF (formerly National Academy Foundation) is an organization whose mission is to bring education, business, and community leaders together to align what is happening in school with future workforce needs. They encourage both local and national businesses to offer hands-on experiences through the power of public and private partnerships. NAF aims to offers a design that integrates with the core high school classes in ways that connect students to future career paths, thus making the coursework highly relevant to them. The organization helps schools create career-themed academies in five general business sectors: hospitality and tourism, finance, information technology, engineering, and health sciences. As of the 2015–2016 school year, they have more than 700 academies in 36 states, serving nearly 90,000 students. Their educational design ignites students' passion for learning and gives businesses the opportunity to shape America's future workforce by transforming the learning environments to include STEM-infused, industry-specific curricula and work-based learning experiences, including internships.

Business partnerships ensure that school curriculum content is current and cultivates the workplace skills of interest and in demand today. Local businesses partner with high schools to support work-based learning activities for teachers, including job-shadowing opportunities, office tours, and exposure to the workplace for students. For eleventh and twelfth graders, companies offer paid internships, with a real paycheck and employer evaluation. This reinforces what students learn in school (L. Dughi, personal communication, August 1, 2016). For students who are financially challenged, getting that paycheck really matters. However, these paid internships are a two-way street. Businesses are quick to acknowledge that although these paid internships begin as philanthropic, they also get a lot back from the innovation of these young people. What better group to bring in and work with on a regular basis than your future users?

In 2014, Lenovo partnered with NAF to launch the Lenovo Scholar Network in 10 NAF academies. It has grown every year and is now reaching more than 50 NAF academies. Lenovo is one company that has helped build public will and understanding in the marketplace that providing work-based learning experiences for students and partnering with high schools is an investment, not an expense. NAF and Lenovo came together at a common place, both striving to offer a high degree of support and value around high school students, with a focus on helping those from low socioeconomic backgrounds have improved career opportunities.

The project supplies students with Lenovo devices and access to the MIT Center for Mobile Learning's App Inventor, a web-based tool for creating Android apps. These are the shiny new materials that schools often believe they can never access because they cost more than most IT budgets can support, and they require coaching in order to use the App Inventor successfully. But in this program, Lenovo supplied the app and the coaching for students, as well as advice for teachers, in order to build a network of knowledge within the broader community. The app development project gives students the opportunity to work in a team, identify a problem, and figure out how to use technology to solve a problem. There is value-based benefit in terms of what Lenovo has done in the app world, which also created great teachable moments for these young people.

The school year culminated in a national competition at which six apps were chosen as winners at the NAF Next 2016 conference. Several of the award-winning apps were tools, like Steps to Success and Student Tracker 9000, that proved students could use their new skills to improve their communities while gaining real-world experience. And from the initial six winners, two fan favorites were announced as well: QMT Translator and Emoji Encouragement (Hoye, 2016). Stories like this show that both students and businesses can benefit from greater collaboration and exposure to one another. Together, NAF and Lenovo designed an innovative way to provide inspiration and Lift to underserved students with the technology and tangible skills needed to succeed in today's workplace.

Instruction IS the Fuel!

Many of the examples of successful schools have come from the NASSP (2011) *Breaking Ranks®* research. These schools focused on developing student-centered culture; collaborative leadership; and aligned curriculum, instruction, and assessment. The principals from all these schools started their turnarounds by getting clear about their own beliefs and creating a compelling vision for what could be possible for their students.

Then they transferred ownership of the vision to the staff and community. This meant developing a new, *shared* mindset among the teachers and parents they served, moving them from using poverty (or stress or boredom) as an excuse for low achievement to seeing students as capable and whole no matter what their ZIP code. This mindset shift was significant to reducing drag.

Next they began a strong, consistent, deep focus on instruction. They created *teacher teams* to look at data, find common trends, and problem solve learning issues that arose. Sometimes they had to create extra classes to get students ready for this more rigorous way of instruction. And sometimes they offered tutoring and additional instructional support outside of class.

They *personalized* instruction for each student. They connected with students, learned what they cared about, and showed that they believed in their dreams for the future. That inspired students to set higher goals for themselves and engage in learning with more effort so they could achieve them. They taught the students that grit and resilience matters and putting forth effort resulted in achieving their goals.

As Hattie (2012) states, there are many teachers who are having significant impact on students in our schools. We can all remember teachers who challenged and inspired us along our educational journey. Schools need to accept Hattie's challenge to have the courage to identify, learn from, and esteem these teachers and invite others to join their ranks, so that they, too, can focus on what matters most and enjoy a similar impact on student achievement.

The principal's role in reducing drag has also changed dramatically. We used to believe the main role of the principal was to be a good manager. He or she did not need to be highly engaged in the process of learning for all. That is, the role was to craft a meaningful vision for the school, provide good building management and orderly discipline, ensure staff had the resources they needed to teach, and send staff to professional learning opportunities that became available during the year. But this limited role is insufficient to ensure that all within the school will have a significant *impact* on student learning. Now the principal's role involves not only these responsibilities but also ensuring teacher effectiveness by activating substantive conversations with teachers that help them reflect on and gain insights about their impact on student learning. This assumes a principal must be conducting frequent observations in classrooms and giving feedback that opens dialogue with faculty about student learning (Smith & Smith, 2015).

An effective principal also must be working to develop the faculty by focusing on *learning* more than teaching. Smith and Smith (2015) underscore that principals should not only be asking teachers what they taught well and not so well; they should also seek feedback *from teachers* about what they know, what they understand, where they have misconceptions, and what would be most helpful as a next step in their own professional learning. In other words, they engage in *dialogue* rather than monologue. The principals do not have to be experts in teaching specific skills and knowledge, but they do need to be the ones who know enough about the learning process to prompt deep thinking and insight with these kinds of conversations. In this way, principals build confidence and competence in the entire staff. They support development of a culture of *professional presence* and *shared responsibility* to help each other bring their "A" game to student learning every day.

To do this well, principals must create an environment in which teachers "feel okay about making mistakes and not knowing, and establish a climate in which (they) welcome error as a learning opportunity" (Smith & Smith, 2015, p. 31). Principals must demonstrate they are active listeners, open to influence, and proficient in creating opportunities for deep dialogue.

Making the System Your Flight Partner

We have spent a lot of time talking about how *schools* reduce drag and become student-centered. But how do school *systems* operate as student-centered? We hear much talk among principals about how

FROM OUR FLIGHT JOURNAL: CAROL HAHN, ELEMENTARY PRINCIPAL, ELLICOTT, MD

Principal as Chief Learner

Carol Hahn, principal at Bellows Spring Elementary School in Ellicott, MD, models the "engaged principal" role. Carol believes that her role as a school leader is to keep her teachers continually learning so that they never lose that sense of what it is like to be a new learner. She sees herself as "Chief Learner" of the school. She observes staff skills and is always scanning the horizon for best practices that have potential to align well with the learning needs of her students. She says, "If I want my teachers to be effective and engaging, what better way to help them than to ensure they are continually new learners themselves!" This creates a pervasive culture within the school of curiosity, risk taking, and errors as opportunities for deeper learning.

Most important, Carol never loses sight of the bigger game. She asks, "What impact is the new resource, instructional practice, or perspective having on student success?" That's the driving question, and she is persistent in asking it of professional learning communities and individual teachers as they conduct data reviews and do individual and team reflection about the impact of the changes. Then she is very careful to share results—whatever they are—and celebrate the learning—whatever they discover (C. Hahn, personal communication, July 7, 2016).

they have to work around the system in order to do things they think are needed for their students. Their attitude is to ask forgiveness rather than seek permission because they fear the district office will block their actions. So Simon and Marceta discussed this issue with Ray Brown, Chief Financial Officer at Prince George's County Public Schools in Maryland. Marceta knew him to be a person who was very focused on providing customer service in his role as head of the district business office.

Ray said that if a district has too many people using workarounds, it's a sign that there is a problem in the business department. He tells his staff that developing positive, trusting relationships with building-level personnel is their highest priority.

> *If the secretary at the school is the one who does the school bookkeeping, then the assistant superintendent of business must be willing to talk directly to her about accounting questions. The assistant superintendent needs to understand it's not a slap*

in the face if the principal refers him to the secretary for these conversations. It's merely a time saver. (R. Brown, personal communication, April 11, 2016)

Ray works hard to instill in their mindset that they are servant leaders—to support and assist the instructional leaders at the schools. He sees the district office role to be acting as *thought partners*—to listen deeply to *understand* academic needs and perspectives and then add value to the solution by offering analytics and perspectives that may be outside the box for principals but valuable in creating the best solution. In the same way, district-level staff must seek input from the building level when making decisions about facilities, maintenance, budget, policies, and procedures. Departments signal their move from a gatekeeper or compliance mentality to a customer service approach when they consistently ask school-level personnel about the impact of changes being proposed and include their ideas in the solution. They begin to model the value of having respectful, partnering relationships at the front end of any work (R. Brown, personal communication, April 11, 2016).

Simon has an example of how changing the way a system is structured can change the behaviors of the people who do the work. He adapted the idea from a participant at a national purchasing conference where he was speaking. He challenged the thousand people in the audience to share how they did something to push themselves out of their comfort zone. Toby Giddings, who worked as a state procurement analyst for the State of Oregon, told about the impact he and his leadership team had when they completely redesigned their organization—the Department of Administrative Services, Procurement Services Office for the State of Oregon. As Simon tells it, the new organizational model became the stickiness that formed cohesion within the culture. It helped people within the organization understand where they fit and what part they played in the mission. They began to understand their contribution in moving the work forward toward customer service.

Before, they had an organizational chart that looked like rows of silos, showing hierarchy and separation. But Toby and his team had an idea for a new chart that would represent how he saw the offices working together, instead of using the classic organizational chart format. What he envisioned he called an "organizational wheel." This wheel removes the perception of hierarchy and separation and replaces it with an illustration of how people work together toward one goal.

Toby's wheel has many layers. Each layer directly supports the next layer and ultimately supports all other layers. The outside of the wheel is the tire—where the rubber hits the road. For him, it is where all the customer centers are. The spokes are the front-line workers and the hub has all the purchasing assistants, managers, and executive support personnel. The direction of the thrust is from the inside out. All workers are supporting the needs of the customers, who are on the outer edge of the tire (T. Giddings, personal communication, February 6, 2014).

Simon wondered whether this model could be applied to schools: If an educational system is to truly receive thrust in the right direction, then the entire way a school is structured must be reevaluated. The direction of the thrust within the system must be from the inside out. That is, student needs, not system perspectives, must be the focus of everyone's work.

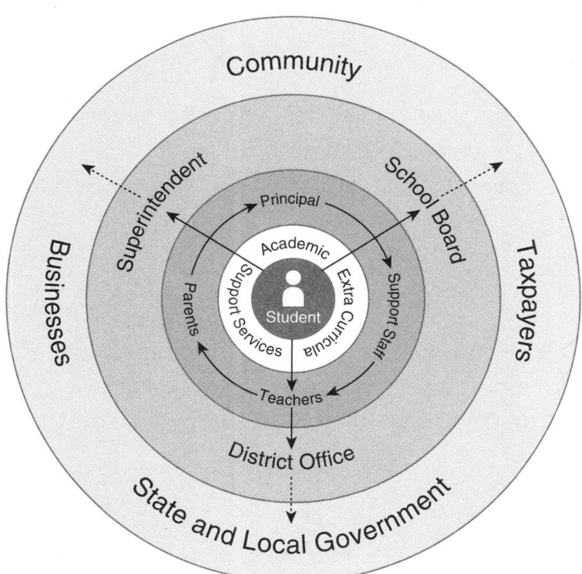

What if the school organizational chart were designed as a wheel instead of a hierarchy?

1. The two outer circles represent entities at the macro level that support the educational system in the community:

   a. state and local government, taxpayers, and businesses;
   b. superintendent, school board, and district office;

2. The next inner circle represents the people directly working with students:
   a. principals;
   b. teachers;
   c. support staff;
   d. parents.

3. The hub represents the services provided that directly support students:
   a. academic content and curriculum;
   b. extracurricular programs and activities;
   c. support services like busing, food service, counseling, etc.

4. The center of the hub is the student, at the axle point where everything supports and adapts to the learning needs of the individual student.

This puts the student at the very center of the educational experience. When all the circles of the wheel and hub are synchronized around individual students, the barrier walls of departments, programs, and scarcity mindset all come tumbling down. Competitiveness within the hub does not serve students well. It's all about serving the needs of individual students—not a class, or program, or department. The entire system works to meet the needs of each student. It's about teams of people working together for a single purpose: to engage every student in learning to his or her full potential. This could become a model for weeding out drag throughout the entire school system and helping every district employee concretely understand their connection and responsibility to students in the classroom.

Call to Action: Assess Your Plan for WOW Student Experiences

These exercises help create WOW (Watch Out, World!) experiences for your students. In the first one, you remember the times when you created a WOW relationship with a student and analyze how you can recreate that experience more often.

Exercise 4.1: Surprise and Delight Teaching Experience

1.	Think of a time when you, as a teacher, experienced an extraordinary student relationship moment—an experience that was above and beyond what you had expected. Describe the experience.	
2.	What was the surprise?	
3.	How did it make you feel?	
4.	What did it make you do?	
5.	How can you create more extraordinary moments like this for other students?	
Share and compare your stories with your team members.		

The next exercise asks you to reflect on how well you and your team are doing in developing student voice in your school.

Exercise 4.2: How Strong Is Student Voice at Your School?

Rate your level of agreement with the statements below on a scale of 1 to 5 (1 = disagree completely and 5 = agree completely). The questions are based on the "Aspirations Framework" by Russ Quaglia (Quaglia & Corso, 2014).

Indicators of Student Self-Worth	**1**	**2**	**3**	**4**	**5**
• Students know they are uniquely valued as members of my class.					
• Students know they can trust me and learn from me.					
• Students know I believe they have the ability to achieve.					
• Students demonstrate a sense of accomplishment when they work hard in my class.					
Indicators of Student Engagement	**1**	**2**	**3**	**4**	**5**
• Students are enthusiastic about their learning.					
• Students are interested in learning new things.					
• Students make effort to do their school work.					
• Students are positive about taking on learning challenges at school and at home.					
Indicators of Student Purpose	**1**	**2**	**3**	**4**	**5**
• Students show accountability for their actions.					
• Students are responsible members of the class.					
• Students dream about their future work and take steps to get there.					

Share your results within your team, then discuss these questions:

1. Is there agreement about the ratings across all classrooms?
2. Where are areas of greatest success?
3. What are deficit areas?
4. Which area does your team consider a priority?
5. Where is there agreement to work together to improve the ratings in that area?
6. How will you measure progress?
7. How will you support each other?
8. What are ways to show personal accountability?

Based on the "Aspirations Framework" by Russ Quaglia.

The final exercise will help you and your team assess whether your school and system structures, policies, and procedures are student, centered.

Exercise 4.3: How Student-Centered Is Your School and Its System?

Have a districtwide internal discussion about these questions. Gather data and input from students, staff, and community members.

- Assess your school according to how well it is meeting the learning needs of students.
    - What data are most important for you to be monitoring?
    - What are the data telling you?
- Assess your school from the perspective of student voice.
    - What are the students telling you about their learning experience at school?
    - How do teachers demonstrate they are student-centered?
    - How does the school respond to student input?
- Assess how well your teacher teams work together to improve student learning.
    - What percentage of team time is spent in conversations about meeting student learning needs?
    - Which of your team's interpersonal skills make team collaboration effective? What may be getting in the way?

(Continued)

Exercise 4.3: (Continued)

  - How engaged and supportive of each other are teachers as they collaborate around instructional impact?

- Rate how well leaders model how they want teachers to treat students.
  - Are leaders walking their talk?

- Assess your system according to the organizational wheel.
  - Is the district office delivering support to the schools for student needs as defined at the school level, or is it focused on bureaucratic compliance instead?
  - In which direction is the thrust flowing?

Visit www.releasingleadershipbrilliance.com to watch the Chapter 4 author video: "How You Can Reduce Drag."

Chapter 5

Breaking Sound Barriers

Be the Impact You Want to See in Schools

It is hard to be an educator today. In the movies we are either portrayed as dolts who haven't got a clue about what is going on with our students, or individual teachers are shown as having to heroically and unrealistically buck the system in order to change lives. Few media stories truly understand the complexity of teaching, and almost none effectively focus on teaching in multicultural classrooms. It's a huge contradiction in our society. Education is perceived as having the potential to powerfully impact children's knowledge and behavior. After all, many advocacy groups want schools to incorporate their teaching materials into the general curriculum—auto safety, fire safety, gun safety, personal finance education, bully proofing, environmental conservation, and the list goes on.

Yet on the other hand, education and the teaching profession are generally devalued. Everybody has an opinion about how to improve the school system because most have gone through it. The millionaires who were high school or college dropouts are held up as models to show that education is not important for success. Simon recalls that when his cousin, Maia Stephen, whom readers met in Chapter 3, announced she wanted to teach in Detroit schools, he was baffled. He thought, "Seriously? Why would anyone do that to themselves?" Simon remembers he couldn't wait to leave Buffalo, New York, which at the time was the second-poorest city in America. Some of the young men with whom he grew up either died early deaths, were on drugs, getting girlfriends pregnant, or in prison. His selfish side wanted to tell Maia that there was more to life than teaching children whom society had written off.

Even Marceta admits to feeling disappointed when her best students say they want to major in education when they go off to college. And then she feels ashamed! To her, the work has been very rewarding because it really *does* make a difference in the lives of so many children. But it's hard work, and it isn't given the appreciation and value that it deserves. Even educators joke among themselves about the value of education and laugh about "going to the dark side" when they move from teacher to principal or principal to district office. It's all very discouraging!

We don't want educators to feel this way. We want them to be proud of their profession and show up every day with confidence and professional presence, knowing that their work is valued and meaningful to society. Educators are shaping the minds of young people who will be leading our society in the future. The importance and efforts of teachers and administrators should not go unnoticed.

We agree that the way educators function in schools *does* need to change because every year our students' needs change and evolve over time. But the change needs to include and build upon the wisdom of educators—not treat them as cogs for others to manipulate. Our purpose for writing *Releasing Leadership Brilliance: Breaking Sound Barriers in Education* was to introduce readers to a framework for transforming themselves and then inviting team members to shift how they see their roles at schools. We want to see them shift from feeling like "just educators" to people who are champions for children and deeply committed to their success, no matter what their ZIP code.

The great majority of schools are doing a good job of meeting the academic and social needs of our children. When people are asked about public education, they are often very critical. But when asked about how they would rate their own neighborhood school, they say it is "good" or "very good." The recent Gallup survey of students shows that more than 50% of them are hopeful about the future and engaged in school (Lopez, 2014). And in this book we have described some outstanding schools that are examples of truly bright spots in our system. Many more exist just like them, but officials simply did not take time to complete the application for recognition or awards.

So while many students are doing well within our educational system, there are also still many who are not. To reach more students and engage them in their own learning is very complex and rigorous work. It involves daunting, adaptive challenges. There are no easy answers or silver bullets.

Aligning With the Breaking Ranks® Framework

When we started this journey of writing *Releasing Leadership Brilliance*, we wanted to provide readers with inspiration to work together in their schools and districts to tackle the hard work of crafting a way forward to greater academic success for more students. We believe the *Breaking Ranks®* research provides a solid framework for doing this work. Its focus on creating a **shared mission and goals** develops the will and grit to stay in the game over the long haul. Its focus on **distributive leadership** invites and empowers educators and staff to broadly take ownership and responsibility for getting the results they want. And its intense focus on **aligning curriculum, instruction, and assessment** puts the emphasis of the work where it matters most—in the classroom.

What *Releasing Leadership Brilliance* adds to this framework is additional concreteness to the process, with stories, research connections, tools, and resources to support and sustain the work.

In Chapter 1, we talked about how to understand and change oneself first and *then* break the sound barriers for the system we are in. Michelangelo said, "I saw the angel in the marble and carved until I set him free." In order to create an authentic, compelling vision for yourself, you have to first understand your own core values and beliefs. This is your **Personal Brilliance**.

Personal Brilliance becomes the compass for how you examine your self-worth, level of engagement, and significance. Before you can show students that they matter, you are invited on a journey to realizing that *you* matter. You really do.

As an educational leader, you are the spark and catalyst to the entire system. Your Personal Brilliance is on daily display because leadership is both caught and taught. Every day you are setting the tone for how teachers teach and how students *want to* learn instead of *have to* learn. The **Weight** of your universal assignment impacts, inspires, and infuses everyone around you.

This can only happen when you are whole in your soul. Being a "whole-person" leader is having an alignment of head, heart, and hands so that the feet around you can follow. At the end of Chapter 1, we suggested several tools to begin this self-discovery work.

In Chapter 2, we presented our belief that *everyone* has a brilliant dream inside to fulfill. So every staff person who works in the school should be on his or her own journey of self-discovery. As a leader you don't just try to sell *your ideas* to everyone else. Your real job is to invite teachers and staff, even parents and community members, on a journey to discover what *they* want for education in *their* community. People learn how to lead based on how they have been taught and led. What are they learning when they watch you?

Once a broad base of people discover who they are at the core, they can create a shared belief in the work. This shared belief has the power to create, inspire, and energize everyone at the school. Teachers pay it forward by engaging students to aspire to uncover their hidden potential. And they create possibilities and solutions for children that would not have been possible without this shared will and commitment. This is the essence of **Collaborative Brilliance.**

Deep self-awareness ("groundedness") allows leaders to connect powerfully with others. These connections create a Boom! that breaks the sound barrier of disengagement and resistance. Collaborative Brilliance creates a **Lift** for everyone on the education continuum and enables them to believe that they have a chance to thrive and be somebody.

Self-discovery and pulling together the shared beliefs of many are steps in creating a shared vision and culture that support broad-based commitment to change. At the end of Chapter 2, we recommended some resources to help you build powerful connections with others in your school and community so together you can develop a shared vision and mission.

Chapter 3 is about **Team Brilliance**. Team Brilliance is leveraging the professional presence within the school to provide **Thrust** for high student achievement. It's having a mindset that focuses on the growth of others and celebrates the gifts that each person brings to the table. It is a mindset that believes working together will create better solutions than working alone. It connects to **distributive or shared leadership** that embodies the second pillar in the *Breaking Ranks®* model.

Hattie (2012) and Hargreave and Fullan (2013) speak about the power of teachers working together in teams to determine their impact on student learning. Pam Robbins (2016) says that the professional context in which teachers work has a profound impact on their ability to respond to the needs of an increasingly diverse student population. Teachers working effectively in teams are a key factor for increasing the number of students who engage in learning.

But, as we learned in Chapter 3, these skills of collaboration and professional presence are rarely taught directly in our college and career classes. The Quaglia Institute for School Voice & Aspirations (2014) issued "The Teacher Voice Report 2010–2014." It found that:

> it is nearly impossible for individuals to reach and sustain their aspirations in a school system in which staff believe they have the ability to be leaders and a desire to participate in decision making, yet feel their opinions are either not sought or when given, go unheeded. Administrators—at all levels—operating in such a system run the risk of confusing conformity with commitment as educators go along to get along and continue to teach as they have always taught (p. 17).

But when faculty, administrators, and staff work together to establish a culture of professional presence within the school, it sets a foundation for the brilliance of all the adults and children in the school to be released. At the end of Chapter 3, we included several tools for helping school leaders analyze staff needs. These can be used to begin meaningful conversations to empower teachers and staff to become partners in making substantive changes to impact student learning.

Then Chapter 4 is the heart of the change process. All the *Breaking Ranks*® principals we interviewed talked about the importance of focusing staff efforts on personalizing instruction for students. We called that **Reducing Drag**. It's about creating caring relationships with students, giving them voice, knowing what they care about and what they aspire to be. Then use curriculum, instruction, and assessment to help students connect their aspirations to the work they are doing in school.

The central work of teachers and administrators is to always be **assessing their impact on student learning**. When they find that students *aren't* engaged in the learning, then the work is figuring out what is needed to invite, excite, and empower students. The most recent report about student voice completed by the Quaglia Institute for School Voice & Student Aspirations (2014) clearly shows the impact of student engagement in learning.

> Engaged students are 16 times more likely to report being academically motivated than students who are not engaged. Finding ways to engage the 40% of students who are not engaged would have a significant impact on their academic motivation. (p. 8)

Whatever we are currently doing with students is not engaging a large sector of them; we need to work *together* to figure out how to meet those needs. Again, the recent student voice report concludes:

> Features of the inherited education model (such as grade-specific instruction, academic tracking, teaching in the silos of the academic disciplines, unidirectional knowledge transfer from teacher to student, time as a constant, etc.) may not adequately suit or serve (a large segment of) the current generation of learners. We believe students' disaffection with school may be less about particular schools, classes, or teachers, and more about the structural underpinnings of an increasingly outdated educational system. . . . If schools are to be places in which teaching and learning thrive and all students are meaningfully engaged, the realities of students' experiences in school must change (p. 16).

How do we begin this transformation? Here's what Robbie Hooker, principal at Clarke Central High School in Georgia whom you met in Chapter 2, recommended when we interviewed him:

> *Utilize the talents you have within their building. Make sure teachers attend conferences and share good practices with their colleagues at the school. Encourage teachers to take risks in finding ways to engage their students. Be transparent in sharing data with faculty. Sometimes the data are not favorable, so use those times to challenge staff to change their instructional practices if they are not effective in improving student learning.* (R. Hooker, personal communication, February 25, 2016)

Hooker also challenges educators to be visible in the community:

> *Make it a priority to visit community centers, especially in public housing areas served by your school. Many of these parents do not feel comfortable visiting the schools. So meet them on their territory, talk to them about school programs, answer their questions, and really bridge the communication gaps. Treat everyone with dignity despite their socioeconomic status, race, or gender. It all builds trust.* (R. Hooker, personal communication, February 25, 2016)

At the end of Chapter 4, we offered several tools to assess system impact on student learning. All the work, at every level, needs to be focused on student learning. It drives the work of individual teachers, curricular departments and student services, schools at every level, and the entire system. Everything needs to focus on student learning. That's our work. That's our promise to the students and their families. That's our mission for the communities and the nation.

The Four Forces Needed to Break Sound Barriers and Fly

So as you reflect on everything that you've read in this book, we want to remind you of several key insights:

Four Cornerstones

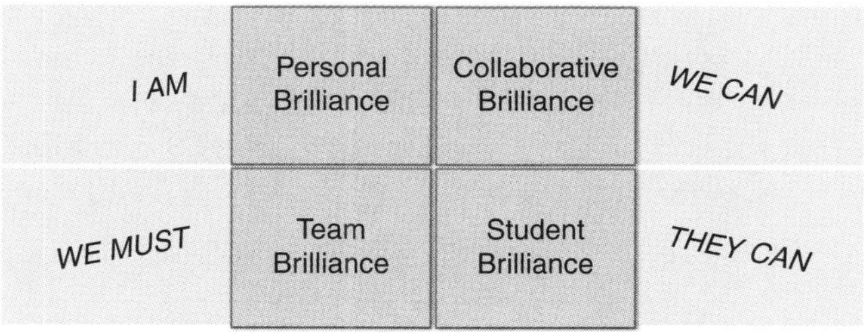

I AM	Personal Brilliance	Collaborative Brilliance	WE CAN
WE MUST	Team Brilliance	Student Brilliance	THEY CAN

- As an educational leader, you are the spark and catalyst to your entire system. Your **Personal Brilliance** is on display every day and it is both caught and taught. The **Weight** and groundedness with which you present yourself is important. So pay attention to how you are showing up!
- **Collaborative Brilliance** is creating a **Lift** that helps connect staff and students to their own inner strengths and values.

Leaders who connect people in this way create the Boom! that breaks the sound barriers of mindless compliance, disillusionment, and resistance. These kinds of leaders invite everyone following them to forward-feed others with curiosity, commitment, and caring about the work of student learning.

- **Team Brilliance** is leveraging the **Thrust** of everyone's potential to move forward. It's adopting a team mindset that focuses on the growth of one another. It celebrates that everyone has something to offer. Each person is respected for his or her strengths and contributions. And working together as a collective is better than working alone. This creates the culture of the school and sets the tone for high professional presence.
- **Student Brilliance** is released when adults in the system become intentional about identifying distractors and demotivators of learning that cause a **Drag** on students. The entire system becomes determined to break the sound barrier of student boredom and disengagement. They work together to begin to equip learners with the grit and resilience to thrive even in very challenging circumstances and aspire to big dreams.

These four cornerstones—personal brilliance, collaborative brilliance, team brilliance, and student brilliance—create a professional presence that enables educators to break the sound barriers of outdated structures and processes within our current educational system. The cornerstones, along with the *Breaking Ranks®* model, give educators a compass and tools to use along the pathway toward transformation.

It is our hope and dream that the ideas we have presented in this book will be a spark to shift educators' thinking about the do-ability of this important work of educational reform. We want to propel them into action that will support them through implementation to the delivery of the promise of education. We can do this work from the inside out!

Visit www.releasingleadershipbrilliance.com to watch the Chapter 5 author video: "How You Can Leverage the Four Cornerstones to Break Sound Barriers."

Are You Ready to Experience the #BreakBarriersTogether Community?

We believe that, as educational leaders, you can transform your school system when you are equipped with the mindset, skillset and toolkit that enables the concepts in *Releasing Leadership Brilliance – Breaking Sound Barriers in Education* to work.

We've created some simple steps to engage you in growing your own professional learning along this pathway.

Step 1:

- Download a copy of the "Starter Guide" that accompanies *Releasing Leadership Brilliance: Breaking Sound Barriers in Education.*
  - Find it on our website: http://ReleasingLeadership-Brilliance.com
  - Use it with colleagues to do book studies and practice sessions.

Step 2:

- Join our ***#BreakBarriersTogether*** exclusive educational community at http://releasingleadershipbrilliance.com
  - Immerse yourself with other educators who are all on the journey to *Releasing Leadership Brilliance;*
  - The group will have access to monthly calls with the authors about implementation topics;

    - Members will share their experiences and have an opportunity to ask questions of the authors and each other; and,
    - Get advance notice of workshops and events coming up to support their implementation efforts.

Step 3:

- Invest in professional development for your school, district, region, or state by hosting a one-day workshop or by gathering your colleagues to join our cohort online course.
    - Contact us through our website to find out what the possibilities might be: www.releasingleadershipbrilliance.com

Step 4:

- Contact us with your questions and success stories to share with others:
    - simon@releasingleadershipbrilliance.com
    - marceta@releasingleadershipbrilliance.com

Bonus—Become a certified coach/facilitator of the *Releasing Leadership Brilliance* Team. This is an exclusive experience and given by invitation only.

Appendix

Exercises to Put *Releasing Leadership Brilliance* Into Practice

This Appendix includes all the exercises from the book. They are tools that Simon and Marceta use to help their clients begin the implementation journey. Use them like a flight plan to get you to the destination of Leadership Brilliance.

We recommend you find a stress-free location away from distractions to do this work. Bring your full presence to it. Let your thinking and feelings emerge to share wisdom with you. Your inner self knows you well, so give it time to speak to you.

Chapter 1: These exercises will help begin your journey of self-discovery so that you recognize your strengths and understand what drives you.

- 1.1: Mining Your Motivator
    - Drill down to find your primary driver.
- 1.2: What Kind of Leader Do I Want to Be?
    - Explore the human characteristics you want to resonate in your work.
- 1.3: Four Cornerstones Worksheet
    - Explore the four key characteristics that you believe create great leadership.

Chapter 2: These exercises will help you consider how to ignite commitment from school staff and engage community support.

- 2.1: "SPARK" Innovation in Your Partnerships
    - Deepen your understanding of why and how you are working with specific partners.

- 2.2: Action Planning for Partners
    - Plan work together as full partners.
- 2.3: Public Agenda Community Conversation Project
    - Get guidance about how to plan and host a conversation event at your school or district.

Chapter 3: These exercises help you assess and develop your team.

- 3.1: Is Your Team an Asset or Liability?
    - Assess the assets of your team and consider how to use them to best advantage.
- 3.2: Skill Versus Will Analysis
    - Analyze individuals based on their skill level and willingness to work with you.
- 3.3: Reframing Complaints
    - Change nagging complaints into learning what people care about underneath them.

Chapter 4: These exercises will help you consider ways to create WOW experiences for students.

- 4.1: Surprise and Delight Teaching Experience
    - Use your own WOW experiences with students to figure out how to recreate them more often.
- 4.2: How Strong Is Student Voice at Your School?
    - Rate how well you and your team are doing in developing student voice at your school.
- 4.3: How Student-Centered Is Your School and Its System?
    - Assess your school system's structures, policies, and procedures for its student-centered perspective.

Exercise 1.1: Mining Your Motivator

Every person is motivated by something in particular. When you know what motivates you, your role becomes more rewarding. You are driven by your passion, and you have a reason for getting out of bed in the morning. This kind of energy is natural and essential for personal success.

But sometimes you can lose sight of what gets you going and find yourself "in the rough." The following exercise will help you drill down on what your primary driver is. Knowing that, you are in a better position to ignite your own brilliance.

Part One

Ask yourself what kinds of drivers, or payoffs, you seek in anything you do. For example, you may get a sense of satisfaction by making a difference, by helping people, or by overcoming barriers to meet a goal.

To get you thinking, review the list of payoffs, or motivators, on the following page, and **circle seven that speak to you** as the ones that impact you most.

Part Two

Review the seven choices you circled and **select the top three** that most motivate you, then record them in the space below.

____

____

____

____

____

____

____

____

____

Examine your top three motivators and **select the one** that you consider your Core Motivator. Record that in the space below.

____

____

____

____

____

____

____

____

____

Adapted from Cheryl Richardson (2005). *Stand Up for Your Life.*

(Continued)

(Exercise 1.1 Continued)

Communicate	Organize	Solve	Collaborate	Achieve
• Inspire	• Achieve	• Confidence	• Connect	• Cause
• Big Picture	• Assemble	• Be Aware	• Bond	• Empower
• Attract	• Accomplish	• Be Present	• Coach	• Increase
• Engage	• Build	• Mutual	• Comfort	• Direct
• Emphasize	• Opportunity	• Courage	• Run	• Excellence
• Reflect	• Ignite	• Impact	• Humor	• Distinguish
• Listen	• Develop	• Elegance	• Congruent	• Encourage
• Entertain	• Prioritize	• Create	• Energy	• Execute
• Enlighten	• Detail-Oriented	• Awareness	• Exhilaration	• Experiment
• Accurate	• Execute	• Honesty	• Unleash	• Risk
• Empathize	• Dedicate	• Improve	• Honor	• Ethical
• Foster	• Invent	• Understand	• In Touch	• Influence
• Complete	• Master	• Recognize	• Integrate	• Imagine
• Truthful	• Integrity	• Earn the Right	• Learn	• Add Value
• Master	• Relevant	• Discover	• Mentor	• Purpose
• Explain	• Create	• New	• Assist	• Accept
• Tell a Story	• Lead	• Opportunity	• Experience	• Challenge
• Visionary	• Quest	• Adjust	• Contribute	• Transform
• Leave a Legacy	• Multitask	• Win-Win	• Appreciate	• Best Practice
		• Forward Momentum		• Make a Difference

Adapted from Cheryl Richardson (2005), *Stand Up for Your Life*. New York, NY: Free Press.

Exercise 1.2: What Kind of Leader Do I Want to Be?

1.	• Why are you doing the work you've chosen to do? (What is your grand purpose?)	
2.	• What is the impact you want to have on your staff and your workplace environment?	
3.	• What concerns do you have when it comes to putting energy into leading a school improvement initiative?	
4.	• What would need to happen with this work for you to consider it a great success?	
5.	• What might stop you from attaining your goals?	
6.	• What is working really well for you right now regarding motivating and inspiring staff?	
7.	• How do you want to show up as the leader you want to be? (What characteristics do you want people to really "get" about you?)	

Exercise 1.3: Four Cornerstone Worksheet

Identify your four "cornerstones" (key characteristics) of great leadership. Then "unpack them" in detail below. Use a separate sheet for each cornerstone. This will help you know what specific skills, behaviors, and attitudes you want to develop.

Name of the Pillar	
Individual Level: How does this cornerstone look, sound, and feel as it is visible in me? What is its impact on me?	
In relationship(s): How does this cornerstone look, sound, and feel as it is visible in relationship with others? What is its impact on the relationship?	
In the broader community: How does this cornerstone look, sound, and feel when it is visible in the broader community? What is its impact on the community?	

Adapted from Jayne Warrilow (http://resonantcoaching.com/).

Exercise 2.1: "SPARK" Innovation in Your Partnerships

Community is to create, shape, and expand the educational experience and impact for students. Innovation-driven partnerships attract and engage people, working together for success of *all* students.

Here are five key question areas your partnership can use to help you focus on your strengths, work collaboratively, and create innovative experiences for students.

S	What is the *synergy* in the partnership that draws you to work for children? The first thing you want to discuss is how you and your partner(s) find meaning in connecting around creating remarkable experiences for students. Briefly remind yourselves that you are in this together. What is each partner's critical role in serving others? How can you leverage this natural synergy?
P	How can we best contribute toward each other's *purpose*? Once you understand where you and your partners synergize, this question lets you and your partner identify expectations and roles. By listening to your partners' responses, you can understand each other's purpose in the student experience. Then clarify and manage how you can help meet each other's objectives. Determine ways in which you can innovate to move beyond today's current situation.
A	What are we hoping to *accomplish*? When you ask this, you and your partner(s) are trying to find out what things are important to each of you, what you are both hoping to accomplish in the way of innovation. Be prepared to ask further questions and clarify each other's understanding so you can know on a deeper level what each of you really needs. As a result, you and your partner(s) will know what is important and what to focus on.
R	What does the ideal *relationship* look like? This question allows you and your partner(s) to describe the kind of working relationship you want to have. Some follow-up questions that can help you: How often should we meet? What is the best way for us to communicate? How do we keep the new ideas flowing? Who else should be involved?
K	How can we *keep* the relationship positive and "for life"? On an ongoing basis, it is a good idea for you to exchange feedback with your partner(s). When you ask this question regularly, you show your partner(s) that you care about their opinions and that you are constantly striving for improvement. Keep each other motivated to continue raising the bar by trying new ideas.

Exercise 2.2: Action Planning for Partners

Use this exercise to help you plan your work together as partners. It makes the work explicit, identifies the key partners needed, and clarifies the greater goal(s) everyone wants.

Use each row to identify the key work for each partner and then use the tool again to plan specific tasks in the partner project.

Example: Summer School Planning

Partner	Share What?	With Whom?	How?	When?	Desired Out-comes?
Sheriff's Office	SRO officers	Summer school staff	Provide classes in bicycle and street safety	Two weeks during summer session	Building relation-ships with local law enforce-ment
Tribal Council	Swimming pool at Boys'/Girls' Club • Free entrance fee • Life-guard	Summer school staff	Provide free daily entry for groups of summer school students	Different groups each day during summer school	Every sum-mer school child gets swim time at least once per week dur-ing the program
Extension Office	Home Economist staff person	Summer school staff	Offer classes in child-care safety and cooking	Two weeks during summer session	Teach self-care and family-support skills to children

Partner	Share What?	With Whom?	How?	When?	Desired Out-comes?

Exercise 2.3: Public Agenda Community Conversation Project

Visit the Public Agenda website here: www.publicagenda.org/pages/choicework-homepage

There are many resources available on this website to help you open up conversations and discussions about topics important to your parents and community members. Under the tab "Our Library," many discussion topics are listed for community conversations. I expanded the K–12 section on the discussion starters webpage and found 19 issues. Below are three examples of the 19 offered by Public Agenda:

- How can we ensure that all children have excellent teachers?
- Creating a formula for success in low-performing schools
- Ready for 21st-century careers

Each discussion starter has three or four typical responses and asks participants to discuss each, weighing the pros and cons for the community. The different perspectives are drawn from what the public thinks about an issue, based on surveys and focus groups, as well as what experts and leaders say about it in policy debates. They are not meant to be definitive but to get the conversation started based on several legitimate perspectives. Such conversations are frequently a solid first step toward new partnerships and initiatives.

Public Agenda's model for Community Conversations encompasses several key principles:

- **Local Nonpartisan Sponsoring Coalition:** A coalition of local organizations and institutions to sponsor and help organize the Community Conversation.
- **Diverse Participants:** Participation that represents a cross section of the community—not just the usual suspects—to ensure that all groups and stakeholders are represented and heard from.
- **Dialogue in Small, Diverse Groups:** Small group discussions facilitated by trained and objective moderators and recorders who document the proceedings for effective follow-up.

Rather than lectures by experts, or gripe sessions by angry constituents, well-designed Community Conversations create a frank, productive problem-solving process in which diverse ideas are put on the table, diverse participants sit at the table, and people work to find common ground and solutions.

Exercise 3.1: Is Your Team an Asset or Liability?

The public today expects high performance from schools, educators, and students. For this reason, our teams need staff at all levels who are assets (people who contribute value) rather than liabilities (people who are disengaged or drawbacks) in planning robust instruction for students.

Are you getting the maximum value from your staff members? Are you tapping into their desire to be high-value assets by using their minds to create greater student engagement and learning?

How can you help them bring more *professional presence* to their teamwork? Help them see the value in being thinking-intensive workers: men and women who use their intangible assets—their knowledge, skills, relationships, and talent—to drive student learning.

Step 1 Think about yourself and your team. List their names or initials below.	**Step 2** List the unique intangible asset (knowledge, skill, talent, etc.) each person can offer the team. Be concise and specific.	**Step 3** As a leader, identify how you can leverage their assets to generate the greatest impact for engaging students with instruction.
NF	Knows how to use guided reading process very effectively.	Ask her to present Guided Reading at a faculty meeting to help move this instructional strategy into more classrooms.
RM	Is excellent in building relationships with challenging young boys.	Ask him to share one of his stories of connecting to a tough kid and explain why he thinks it worked with the student. Then ask him to apply this insight to setting higher learning expectations for young boys.

Exercise 3.2: Skill Versus Will Analysis

The Skill Versus Will matrix helps answer two simple yet important questions:

- How much can the person rely on his or her skills to complete the task?
- How much does that person really want to complete the task?

Analyze your staff using our Skill Versus Will model. How can this data help you tailor your conversations with individual faculty members? Who are the people in the high skill/high will quadrant whom you could tap for more leadership responsibility?

Think about two or three teachers you are currently working with. Analyze where they might be on the model. How could this model help you to work with these individuals?

High Will	**GUIDE** • Offer low-risk opportunities to grow and learn. • Provide tools, training, coaching, and feedback about what they are doing well. • Relax judgment and control as you recognize progress.	**DELEGATE** • Recognize them and communicate your trust in them. • Help them develop stretch goals, broaden their responsibilities, and treat them as "partners." • Give broad latitude for them to experiment, allowing them to share their experiences and mentor others. • Help them become the shapers of the culture.
Low Will	**DIRECT** • Get to know individuals personally and assume positive intent. • Help them create a vision for their work. • Structure quick wins, train/coach patiently, supervise with frequent feedback about the progress you see, and set clear expectations.	**EXCITE** • Get to know individuals personally, what motivates them, and the values to which they aspire. • Seek to understand "why" they have low will. • Help them reconnect to what drew them into education in the first place. • Look for and provide recognition to reinforce their positive behaviors.
	Low Skill	**High Skill**

Adapted from Landsberg, M. (2009). *The Tao of Coaching*. London: Profile Books.

Exercise 3.3: Reframing Complaints

When you are faced with a recurring complaint from your staff, parents, or community, use this exercise to figure out what people are really asking for underneath the surface words. It will help you address what they care about when you respond, instead of getting into a debate about the complaint on the surface.

Think about a person (colleague, school parent, friend, or family member) who is always complaining to you about an issue.

Column 1	Column 2	Column 3	Column 4	Column 5
Exact words	**Underlying worry/fear**	**Care about?**	**Where is the win-win (sweet spot)?**	**How to start?**
What are some of the exact words the person uses in the complaint?	Think deeply about what could be the underlying fear, worry, or emotion that is really behind the concern.	Flip the fear, worry, or emotion to create a positive statement about what the person cares about.	What does this tell you about a strength or positive characteristic the person has that you could also agree with?	What is a way to start a conversation, seeing the complainer as having a legitimate perspective, and speaking about what he *really* cares about?
Student failed a test: "worked hard, teacher isn't any good, child very discouraged, wants to drop the class or change teachers."	*Parent wants child to do well in school. Fear that teacher doesn't like his child so not being fair.*	*Parent cares that his child and teacher have a strong, positive relationship. (Wants teacher to love his child as much as he does.)*	*He understands the importance of having a strong, positive relationship with teachers.* *Sweet spot is focusing on building that relationship.*	*"I hear the frustration in your voice and I'm wondering if you are really worrying that the teacher doesn't like your child."*

(Continued)

(Exercise 3.3 Continued)

Column 1	Column 2	Column 3	Column 4	Column 5
Exact words	**Underlying worry/fear**	**Care about?**	**Where is the win-win (sweet spot)?**	**How to start?**

Exercise 4.1: Surprise and Delight Teaching Experience

1. Think of a time when you, as a teacher, experienced an extraordinary student relationship moment—an experience that was above and beyond what you had expected. Describe the experience below.

2. What was the surprise?

3. How did it make you feel?

4. What did it make you do?

5. How can you create more extraordinary moments like this for other students?

Share and compare your stories with your team members.

Exercise 4.2: How Strong Is Student Voice at Your School?

Rate your level of agreement with the statements below on a scale of 1 to 5 (1 = disagree completely and 5 = agree completely). The questions are based on the "Aspirations Framework" by Russ Quaglia (Quaglia & Corso, 2014).

Indicators of Student Self-Worth	**1**	**2**	**3**	**4**	**5**
• Students know they are uniquely valued as members of my class.					
• Students know they can trust me and learn from me.					
• Students know I believe they have the ability to achieve.					
• Students demonstrate a sense of accomplishment when they work hard in my class.					
Indicators of Student Engagement	**1**	**2**	**3**	**4**	**5**
• Students are enthusiastic about their learning.					
• Students are interested in learning new things.					
• Students make effort to do their school work.					
• Students are positive about taking on learning challenges at school and at home.					
Indicators of Student Purpose	**1**	**2**	**3**	**4**	**5**
• Students show accountability for their actions.					
• Students are responsible members of the class.					
• Students dream about their future work and take steps to get there.					

Share your results within your team, then discuss these questions:

1. Is there agreement about the ratings across all classrooms?
2. Where are areas of greatest success?

3. What are deficit areas?
4. Which area does your team consider a priority?
5. Where is there agreement to work together to improve the ratings in that area?
6. How will you measure progress?
7. How will you support each other?
8. What are ways to show personal accountability?

Based on the "Aspirations Framework" by Russ Quaglia.

Exercise 4.3: How Student-Centered Is Your School and Its System?

Have a districtwide internal discussion about these questions. Gather data and input from students, staff, and community members.

- Assess your school according to how well it is meeting the learning needs of students.
  - What data are most important for you to be monitoring?
  - What are the data telling you?
- Assess your school from the perspective of student voice.
  - What are the students telling you about their learning experience at school?
  - How do teachers demonstrate they are student-centered?
  - How does the school respond to student input?
- Assess how well your teacher teams work together to improve student learning.
  - What percentage of team time is spent in conversations about meeting student learning needs?
  - Which of your team's interpersonal skills make team collaboration effective? What may be getting in the way?
  - How engaged and supportive of each other are teachers as they collaborate around instructional impact?
- Rate how well leaders model how they want teachers to treat students.
  - Are leaders walking their talk?
- Assess your system according to the organizational wheel.
  - Is the district office delivering support to the schools for student needs as defined at the school level, or is it focused on bureaucratic compliance instead?
  - In which direction is the thrust flowing?

Recommended Reading

There were several books that influenced our writing of *Releasing Leadership Brilliance: Breaking Sound Barriers in Education,* and we want to share just a few with you.

Release Your Brilliance: The 4 Steps to Transforming Your Life and Revealing Your Genius to the World by Simon T. Bailey. You will learn why a job is what you are paid to do, but Release Your Brilliance is what you are made to do. Everyone is a diamond and they are formed through heat, pressure, and change. This book is the catalyst and foundation for writing *Releasing Leadership Brilliance.* Thank you, Corwin.

Coaching Conversations: Transforming Your School One Conversation at a Time by Linda M. Gross Cheliotes and Marceta F. Reilly. This book introduces educational leaders to essential communication skills—committed listening, positive intention, powerful questioning, and reflective feedback. These skills remind us to be mindful of the power of words and how they shape minds.

Student Voice: The Instrument of Change by Russell J. Quaglia and Michael J. Corso. Russell and Michael have written a provocative book. Their research simply proves that meaningful school reform starts with the most powerful partners—your students. They also give you a thorough blueprint for engaging students.

More Courageous Conversations About Race by Glenn Singleton. Race is often the last conversation that people, let alone educators, ever want to have. When we were writing our book, Glenn was the catalyst that challenged us not to tip-toe through the tulips about race in education. He provided us with keen insight on how to move conversations beyond black and white. You will learn a framework for achieving racial equity in education. We encourage you to read it and pass it on.

In his previous book, *Courageous Conversations About Race*, Singleton cites grim statistics about the impact of race on student achievement. College Board SAT data show white students outperformed black and brown students at every income level, and black students are the lowest performing group at every income level. There is even achievement disparity between black and white students who are equally poor. And poorer white students actually outperformed middle income black and brown students.

Visible Learning for Teachers by John Hattie. This is a classic must-read for educators who are serious about sustainable transformation in their school. This is one of the books that you read, share, pass on, and then go back and read it again. This is like going back for seconds after a really good meal.

Evaluating Instructional Leadership: Recognized Practices for Success by Julie and Raymond Smith. When we first met Julie and Raymond Smith, we knew that we were in the presence of dynamic educators. Their combined 70+ years of educational wisdom is distilled down into nine chapters that focus on effectiveness, applicability, and deliberate practice.

Deliberate Optimism: Reclaiming the Joy in Education by Debbie Silver, Jack Berckemeyer, and Judith Baenen. The title alone sums up why this is one of our favorite books. Just like a skillful surgeon, the authors equip teachers with five tried-and-true principles on how to be deliberate. You will love Chapter 3. It's almost as if the authors are living in our head as educators.

The Multigenerational Workplace by Jennifer Abrams and Valerie Von Frank. We love the deep-dive insight on how to be generationally savvy. The research, simplicity, and applicable steps are critical to implementing their wisdom.

The End of Average: How We Succeed in a World That Values Sameness by Todd Rose. Hands down, this has to be one of the most important books to read right now. A friend told me about it, and I told

Marceta about it, and on and on. One of my favorite quotes in the book: "In school, you are graded and ranked by comparing your performance to the average student." Todd Rose is the director of the Mind, Brain, and Education program at Harvard Graduate School of Education.

World Class Learners: Educating Creative and Entrepreneurial Students by Yong Zhao. As entrepreneurs, we love this book. Yong is a professor/researcher who unlocks the secrets to cultivating independent thinkers who will think differently about creating jobs and solving some of the world's biggest problems.

Mindsets and Moves: Strategies That Help Readers Take Charge, Grades 1–8 by Gravity Goldberg. This is one of our favorite reads. Gravity highlights key ways for teachers to examine their roles in impacting the reader. I like the insight on how to be a miner, mirror, model, and mentor.

Optimize Your School: It's All About Strategy by Lyle Leon Jenkins. The insight in this book is profound. We love that Lyle added "strategic thinking" to the continuous improvement model.

Leadership Coaching for Educators: Bringing Out the Best in School Administrators by Karla Reiss. This book masterfully lays out the case for coaching in the educational space. You can discover how the Colorado Association of School Executives, Wisconsin Association of School District Administrators, and Georgia School Superintendents Association leverage coaching.

High Impact Instruction: A Framework for Great Teaching by Jim Knight. This is the gold standard for how to teach effectively. Any teacher who is serious about influencing her students long-term needs to have this book.

Partnering With Students: Building Ownership of Learning by Mary J. O'Connell and Kara Vandas. We really like this step-by-step guide about building learning capacity and creating a classroom culture in which students take the lead.

The Principal's Companion: Strategies to Lead Schools for Student and Teacher Success by Pamela M. Robbins and Harvey Alvy. This commonsense approach to being a learning leader is refreshing. One of our favorite chapters is about effectively working with the central office to coordinate teaching, learning, and professional development.

Quality Questioning: Research-Based Practice to Engage Every Learner by Jackie Walsh and Beth Sattes. In any educational situation, there is often the need to ask a quantity of questions. However, Jackie and Beth provide us with the understanding that questions can trigger thinking, transform schools, and enrich your professional development journey.

Bibliography

Introduction

Bailey, S. (2008). *Release your brilliance*. New York, NY: HarperCollins.

Gross Cheliotes, L., & Reilly, M. F. (2010). *Coaching conversations: Transforming your school one conversation at a time*. Thousand Oaks, CA: Corwin.

McGregor, J. (2015, March 31). Zappos to employees: Get behind our "no bosses" approach or leave with severance. *Washington Post*. Retrieved from https://www.washingtonpost.com/news/on-leadership/wp/2015/12/01/tony-hsieh-got-rid-of-bosses-at-zappos-and-thats-not-even-his-biggest-idea/

McIntosh, R. (2007). *The greatest secret: God's law of attraction for lasting happiness, fulfillment, health, and abundance in life*. Lakeland, FL: White Stone Books.

Reingold, J. (2016, March 4). The Zappos experiment. *Fortune*. Retrieved from http://fortune.com/zappos-tony-hsieh-holacracy/

Robinson, Sir K. (2013) How to escape education's death valley. *TED Talks Education*. Retrieved from https://www.ted.com/talks/ken_robinson_how_to_escape_education_s_death_valley?language=en

Chapter 1

Clifton, J. (2011). *The coming jobs war*. Washington, DC: Gallup Press.

della Cava, M. (2012, December 6). Chuck Yeager, still soaring at 89. *USA Today*. Retrieved from http://www.usatoday.com/story/life/tv/2012/12/05/chuck-yeager-intervew/1695301/

Dweck, C. (2006). *Mindset: The new psychology of success.* New York, NY: Random House.

Fullan, M. (2005). *Leadership and sustainability: Systems thinkers in action.* Thousand Oaks, CA: Corwin.

Ginott, H. (1972). *Teacher and child.* New York, NY: Macmillan.

Marzano, R., Waters, T., & McNulty, B. A. (2005). *School leadership that works: From research to results.* Alexandria, VA: ASCD.

National Association of Secondary School Principals. (2011). *Breaking ranks: The comprehensive framework for school improvement.* Reston, VA: Author.

Richardson, C. (2005). *Stand up for your life.* New York, NY: Free Press.

Robinson, Sir K. (2013, April). How to escape education's death valley. *TED Talks Education.* Retrieved from https://www.ted.com/talks/ken_robinson_how_to_escape_education_s_death_valley?language=en

Rossmann, T. (2002, March 22). What happens when an aircraft breaks the sound barrier? *Scientific American.* Retrieved from https://www.scientificamerican.com/article/what-happens-when-an-airc/

Seashore Louis, K., & Wahlstrom, K. (2011). Principals as cultural leaders. *Phi Delta Kappan, 92*(5), 52–56.

Woodson, C. G. (2008). *The mis-education of the negro.* Radford, VA: Wilder.

Chapter 2

Adler University. (2011, September 25). Reflection on Bielby lecture: Is any company immune to unconscious bias? *The Socially Responsible Practitioner.* Retrieved from http://www.adler.edu/blog/reflection-on-bielby-lecture-is-any-company-immune-to-unconscious-bias

Anderson, K. (2016, June 3). St. Louis area superintendent shares ideas for improving Hamilton County's struggling schools. *Chattanooga Times Free Press.* Retrieved from http://www.timesfreepress.com/news/local/story/2016/jun/03/solutions-success-superintendent-shares-ideim/369152/

Bronner, D. (2015). *Change your trajectory: Make the rest of your life better*. New Kensington, PA: Whitaker House.

Brown, E. (2015, September 15). Laurene Powell Jobs donates $50 million to redesign high school. *The Washington Post*. Retrieved from https://www.washingtonpost.com/local/education/laurene-powell-jobs-donates-50-million-to-redesign-high-school/2015/09/15/9d234458-5b01-11e5-b38e-06883aacba64_story.html

Drucker, P. (1995). *Management: Tasks, responsibilities, practices*. Retrieved from http://www.icmbpl.com/Management%20-%20Tasks,%20Responsibilities,%20Practices%20by%20Peter%20Drucker%20e%20book.pdf

Gerson, M. (2015, December 29). Education pact comes at cost. *Topeka Capital-Journal*, p. 4.

Huffington, A.(2010). *Third world America: How our politicians are abandoning the middle class and betraying the American Dream*. Old Saybrook, CT: Tantor Media.

Ismail, S., Malone, M. S., & van Geest, Y. (2014). *Exponential organizations: Why new organizations are ten times better, faster, and cheaper than yours (and what you can do about it)*. New York, NY: Diversion Books.

Liedtke, M. (2015, October 27). Oracle to build high school on its Silicon Valley campus. *Los Angeles Times*. Retrieved from http://www.latimes.com/business/technology/la-fi-oracle-high-school-20151027-story.html

Mero, D., & Hartzman, M. (2012). *Breaking ranks in action: Collaboration is the foundation*. Retrieved from https://nassp.org/

National Association of Secondary School Principals. (2011). *Breaking ranks: The comprehensive framework for school improvement*. Reston, VA: Author.

Public Agenda. (2016). http://www.publicagenda.org/

Rourke, J., & Boone, E. (2014). *Collaboration: The driving force for success*. Retrieved from https://nassp.org/

Singleton, G. (2015). *Courageous conversations about race: A field guide for achieving equity in schools* (2nd ed.). Thousand Oaks, CA: Corwin.

Wiseman, L., & McKeown, G. (2010). *Multipliers: How the best leaders make everyone smarter*. New York, NY: HarperCollins.

Chapter 3

Asa, R. (2015, December 15). Digital learning innovator works to reimagine future of education. *Chicago Tribune*. Retrieved from http://www.chicagotribune.com/lifestyles/ct-constance-yowell-digital-learning-family-1227-20151215-story.html

Drago-Severson, E. (2008). 4 practices serve as pillars for adult learning. *The Journal of Staff Development, 29*(4), 60–63.

Hargreaves, A., & Fullan, M. (2013). The power of professional capital. *Journal of Staff Development, 34*(3), 36–39.

Landsberg, M. (2009). *The Tao of coaching: Boost your effectiveness at work by inspiring and developing those around you*. London, UK: Profile Books.

Leana, C. R. (2011). The missing link in school reform. *Stanford Social Innovation Review, 9*(4), 34.

Newton-Carroll, S. (2016). *Every student succeeds: The Breakthrough School way*. Presentation at NASSP Conference, February 25, Orlando, FL.

Rock, D. (2008). SCARF: A brain-based model for collaborating with and influencing others. *The NeuroLeadership Journal, 1*, 1–8.

Sparks, D. (2002). Inner conflicts, inner strengths. *Journal of Staff Development, Summer*, 66–71.

Wilson, L., & Wilson, H. (2004). *Play to win: Choosing growth over fear in work and life*. Austin, TX: Bard Press.

Chapter 4

Duckworth, A. (2013). Grit: The power of passion and perseverance. *TED Talks Education*. Retrieved from https://www.ted.com/talks/angela_lee_duckworth_grit_the_power_of_passion_and_perseverance

Dweck, C. (2006). *Mindset: The new psychology of success*. New York: Ballantine Books.

Goldberg, G. (2016). *Mindsets and moves: Strategies that help readers take charge*. Thousand Oaks, CA: Corwin.

Goodwin, B., & Miller, K. (2013) Research says grit plus talent equals student success. *Educational Leadership, 71*(1), 74–76.

Hattie, J. (2012). *Visible learning for teachers: Maximizing impact on learning*. Thousand Oaks, CA: Corwin.

Hoye, J. D. (2016). NAF and Lenovo: Strengthening the talent pipeline. *NAF Now*. Retrieved from http://naf.org/news_articles/naf-lenovo-strengthening-the-talent-pipeline

Leana, C. R. (2011). The missing link in school reform. *Stanford Social Innovation Review, 9*(4), 34.

Lopez, S. (2014). Not enough students are success-ready. *Gallup*. Retrieved from http://www.gallup.com/businessjournal/168242/not-enough-students-success-ready.aspx

Quaglia, R. J., & Corso, M. J. (2014). *Student voice: The instrument for change*. Thousand Oaks, CA: Corwin.

Sagor, R. (1996). Building resiliency in students. *Educational Leadership, 54*(1), 38–43.

Smith, J. R., & Smith, R. L. (2015). *Evaluating instructional leadership: Recognized practices for success*. Thousand Oaks, CA: Corwin.

Zhao, Y. (2012). *World class learners: Educating creative and entrepreneurial students*. Thousand Oaks, CA: Corwin.

Chapter 5

Hargreaves, A., & Fullan, M. (2013). The power of professional capital. *Journal of Staff Development, 34*(3), 36–39.

Hattie, J. (2012). *Visible learning for teachers: Maximizing impact on learning*. Thousand Oaks, CA: Corwin.

Lopez, S. (2014). Not enough students are success-ready. *Gallup*. Retrieved from http://www.gallup.com/businessjournal/168242/not-enough-students-success-ready.aspx

Phillips, M. (2016, February 22). The class—a film to teach and inspire [blog post]. *Edutopia*. Retrieved from https://www.edutopia.org/blogs

Quaglia Institute for School Voice & Student Aspirations. (2014a). *My voice: National student report 2014 (Grades 6–12)*. Portland, ME: Author.

Quaglia Institute for School Voice & Student Aspirations. (2014b). *Teacher voice: Report 2010–2014*. Portland, ME: Author.

Robbins, P. (2016). *A leadership conversation: Creating a context for professional learning and student growth.* Presentation at the 3rd Annual Corwin Author Consulting Retreat, January, 2016.

Index